MODERN WORLD CULTURES

Africa South of the Sahara

◆

Australia and the Pacific

◆

East Asia

◆

Europe

◆

Latin America

◆

North Africa and the Middle East

◆

Northern America

◆

Russia and
the Former Soviet Republics

◆

South Asia

◆

Southeast Asia

◆

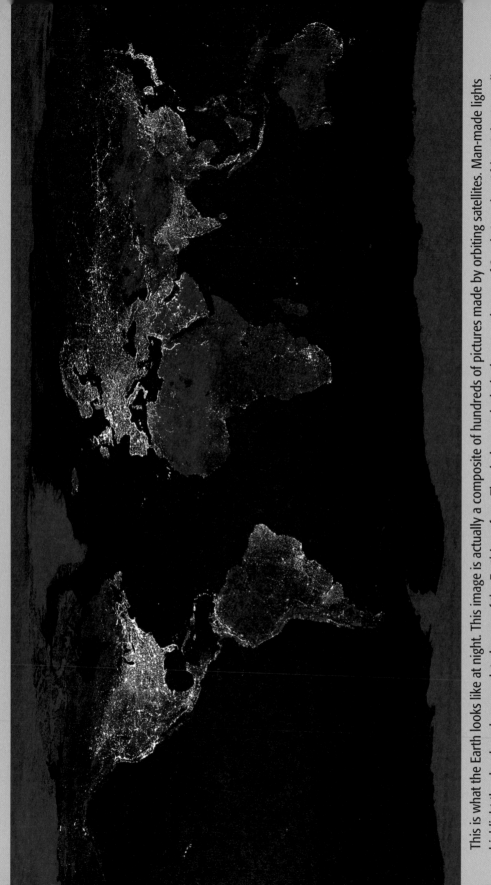

This is what the Earth looks like at night. This image is actually a composite of hundreds of pictures made by orbiting satellites. Man-made lights highlight the developed or populated areas of the Earth's surface. The dark areas include the central parts of South America, Africa, Asia, Australia, and the polar regions.

Cronin

Latin America

Charles F. Gritzner
South Dakota State University

CHELSEA HOUSE
PUBLISHERS
An imprint of Infobase Publishing

Cover: Plaza de Armas and San Francisco de Arequipa Cathedral, Peru.

Latin America

Copyright © 2006 by Infobase Publishing

Chelsea House
An imprint of Infobase Publishing
132 West 31st Street
New York NY 10001

Library of Congress Cataloging-in-Publication Data

Gritzner, Charles F.
  Latin America / Charles F. Gritzner.
    p. cm. — (Modern world cultures)
  Includes bibliographical references and index.
  ISBN 0-7910-8142-7 (hard cover)
  1. Latin America—Juvenile literature. I. Title. II. Series.
  Republic—Biography—Juvenile literature. I. Title. II. Series.
  F1408.2.G75 2006
  980—dc22   2005032686

Chelsea House books are available at special discounts when purchased in bulk quantities for businesses, associations, institutions, or sales promotions. Please call our Special Sales Department in New York at (212) 967-8800 or (800) 322-8755.

You can find Chelsea House on the World Wide Web at http://www.chelseahouse.com

Text and cover design by Takeshi Takahashi

Printed in the United States of America

Bang MCC 10 9 8 7 6 5 4 3 2 1

This book is printed on acid-free paper.

All links and web addresses were checked and verified to be correct at the time of publication. Because of the dynamic nature of the web, some addresses and links may have changed since publication and may no longer be valid.

TABLE OF CONTENTS

Charles F. Gritzner

Geography is the key that unlocks the door to the world's wonders. There are, of course, many ways of viewing the world and its diverse physical and human features. In this series—MODERN WORLD CULTURES—the emphasis is on people and their cultures. As you step through the geographic door into the ten world cultures covered in this series, you will come to better know, understand, and appreciate the world's mosaic of peoples and how they live. You will see how different peoples adapt to, use, and change their natural environments. And you will be amazed at the vast differences in thinking, doing, and living practiced around the world. The MODERN WORLD CULTURES series was developed in response to many requests from librarians and teachers throughout the United States and Canada.

As you begin your reading tour of the world's major cultures, it is important that you understand three terms that are used throughout the series: geography, culture, and region. These words and their meanings are often misunderstood. **Geography** is an age-old way of viewing the varied features of Earth's surface. In fact, it is the oldest of the existing sciences! People have always had a need to know about and understand their surroundings. In times past, a people's world was their immediate surroundings; today, our world is global in scope. Events occuring half a world away can and often do have an immediate impact on our lives. If we, either individually or as a nation of peoples, are to be successful in the global community, it is essential that we know and understand our neighbors, regardless of who they are or where they may live.

Geography and history are similar in many ways; both are methodologies—distinct ways of viewing things and events. Historians are concerned with time, or when events happened. Geographers, on the other hand, are concerned with space, or where things are located. In essence, geographers ask: "What is where, why there, and why care?" in regard to various physical and human features of Earth's surface.

Culture has many definitions. For this series and for most geographers and anthropologists, it refers to a people's way of life. This means the totality of everything we possess because we are human, such as our ideas, beliefs, and customs, including language, religious beliefs, and all knowledge. Tools and skills also are an important aspect of culture. Different cultures, after all, have different types of technology and levels of technological attainment that they can use in performing various tasks. Finally, culture includes social interactions—the ways different people interact with one another individually and as groups.

Finally, the idea of **region** is one geographers use to organize and analyze geographic information spatially. A region is an area that is set apart from others on the basis of one or more unifying elements. Language, religion, and major types of economic activity are traits that often are used by geographers to separate one region from another. Most geographers, for example, see a cultural division between Northern, or Anglo, America and Latin America. That "line" is usually drawn at the U.S.–Mexico boundary, although there is a broad area of transition and no actual cultural line exists.

The ten culture regions presented in this series have been selected on the basis of their individuality, or uniqueness. As you tour the world's culture realms, you will learn something of their natural environment, history, and way of living. You will also learn about their population and settlement, how they govern themselves, and how they make their living. Finally, you will take a peek into the future in the hope of identifying each region's challenges and prospects. Enjoy your trip!

Charles F. Gritzner
Department of Geography
South Dakota State University
May 2005

CHAPTER 1

Introducing Our Latin American Neighbors

Welcome to Latin America, one of the world's largest, most homogeneous, and most fascinating culture realms! Strangely, most of us *norteamericanos* (Northern Americans, or residents of Canada and the United States) know very little about our southern neighbors. Sadly, too, much of what we do "know" about the region is false. Stereotypes, misconceptions, and general ignorance abound. Mexican writer Carlos Fuentes once said, "What the United States does best is to understand itself. What it does worst is understand others." To understand other places and people, we must learn about them. Yet former *New York Times* editor and columnist James Reston once noted that "Somehow the people of the United States will do anything for Latin America except read about it." In this book, the author attempts to provide the reader with a glimpse of the *real* Latin America. When you have completed your journey, he hopes that you share his deep affection for this dynamic, fascinating, and diverse region and its more than one-half billion people.

There are many reasons why it is important for Northern Americans to understand Latin America. The most obvious, perhaps, is that we are neighbors, sharing the huge landmass called America that occupies much of the Western Hemisphere. Economically, in terms of labor, resources, manufacturing, and tourism, ties between the two regions are strengthening rapidly. Political instability in Latin America can have a profound impact on Northern America. Much of the international drug trade originates in Latin America. Today, people of Latin American ancestry are the leading and most rapidly growing "minority" population in the United States. In addition, Northern American culture is increasingly showing a strong Latin imprint. Many Northern Americans enjoy Mexican food, and Mexican tequila has become a popular alcoholic beverage. As baseball fans, we cheer for dozens of players from the Dominican Republic, Puerto Rico, Venezuela, and other south-of-the-border locales. Calypso, reggae, mariachi, and salsa are just some of Latin America's contributions to the music many of us enjoy. These are just a few of the strong and rapidly growing ties that exist between Northern and Latin America.

HEMISPHERIC REGIONAL DIVISIONS

Cultural regions are often difficult to define. Perhaps it is best to think of them as "convenience packages." Geographers use the concept to divide Earth's surface into manageable units of space. Clearly, the way of living in the United States and Canada differs somewhat from that of Mexico and Brazil. Today, the culture in both regions is predominantly European in origin, yet many differences exist. Through time, geographers and others have divided America into a number of different regions. Today, however, the most widely used division is Northern (or Anglo) America and Latin America. This is the division used in the MODERN WORLD CULTURES series and in this book. Some confusion exists in regard to the terms and areas associated with the hemisphere's regional divisions, however. Several terms and the areas to which they correctly relate follow.

North America and **South America** are *continents*. They are physically separated by the Isthmus of Panama (which coincides with the route of the Panama Canal). For purposes of statistical convenience (as in most textbooks), the boundary is often placed at the political boundary between Panama and Colombia. (A word of caution: Today, *North America* is often used incorrectly in place of Anglo America, or predominantly English-speaking United States and Canada).

Northern (Anglo) America and **Latin America** are *culture* regions. Because they occur as broad zones of transition, it is difficult to draw a sharp line that divides the two culture realms. Traditionally, the line dividing Northern and Latin America has been placed at the border of the United States and Mexico. Within the two regions, of course, there exists tremendous cultural diversity. This is one problem geographers face when attempting to delineate regions. Regions must be thought of as generalizations within which there are always exceptions. In Latin America, for example, there are small populations that speak English, Dutch, French, and various *Amerindian* (American Indian), or other languages. Most people speak Spanish or Portuguese (in Brazil), both of which are Latin-derived Romance tongues.

Middle, Central, and Caribbean America are popular regions widely recognized by local inhabitants, businesses, scholars, and others. *Middle America* is that part of Latin America located on the North American continent. It extends

The continent of South America is separated from North America by the Isthmus of Panama. The topography of the world's fourth-largest continent varies from the rugged Andes Mountains, which extend the length of the continent in the west, to eastern Argentina's fertile Pampas region.

from the U.S.–Mexico border southward to the border between Panama and Colombia. As such, it includes both Central and Caribbean America. *Central America* includes those countries that often are referred to as the "Banana Republics." The region includes all territory on the North American mainland southward from southern Mexico. Finally, *Caribbean America* is a loosely defined region most commonly used in reference to those islands in and countries immediately surrounding the Caribbean Sea.

THE AMERICAS: SIMILARITIES AND CONTRASTS

Northern (Anglo) and Latin America have many things in common. Both were "discovered" by Europeans about 500 years ago. The European voyages of discovery began with Columbus's landfall in 1492. Settlers soon followed in the wake of European explorers. What began as a mere trickle rapidly became a flood of humanity that often washed away and destroyed native peoples and their ways of living. This huge migration of peoples and the resulting relocation diffusion (spread) of culture is recognized as the New World Revolution. The resulting clash of cultures and civilizations proved to be one of the most dramatic cultural events in all of history. In the period of a few centuries, European culture— Northwest European in Northern America and Iberian (Spain and Portugal) in Latin America—largely replaced native ways of living. Its impact continues to be felt throughout much of the Americas even today.

The two Americas share many other things, as well. Both, for example, have relatively low populations and population densities. Each has huge areas of land that are suitable for settlement and economic development. Many sharp differences also exist, however, thereby justifying the division of the American landmass into two distinct culture realms. Major cultural contrasts will be discussed in detail in their appropriate context throughout the book. Briefly, they include:

Northern America	Latin America
• Dominantly of Northwest European culture	• Dominantly of Iberian culture
• Primarily English-speaking	• Primarily Spanish- and Portuguese-speaking
• Protestant and Catholic	• Primarily Roman Catholic
• Few Native Americans	• Large Amerindian population
• Urban and industrial	• Urban, but lacking adequate economic base
• Economic and political stability	• Lacking institutional stability
• Immigrants came to settle permanently and sink roots	• Immigrants came to exploit and return to homeland (although most never did)
• Protestant work ethic (honor in labor)	• Manual labor (at least initially) seen as demeaning

LATIN AMERICAN UNITY

There are 20 Latin American countries on the continental mainland and nearly as many independent states or possessions in the Caribbean. Despite the many similarities between countries, each is different in some way. Latin Americans are highly individualistic and fiercely independent. For this reason, regional linkages between and among countries has been very slow in developing. Latin America's history has been marked by conflict to a much greater extent than it has by harmony and cooperation among states.

Chilean Nobel Laureate Gabriela Mistral once suggested that "What unites us in Spanish America is our beautiful language and our distrust of the United States." More than six decades later, Mistral's words still ring true in many respects. Many other traits, some already mentioned, serve as ties that bind the region together, however. Obviously, the region is unified by location, culture, and history. Much of the region also shares common problems.

Crime and corruption are widespread, as is continuing civil conflict involving terrorist groups, drug cartels, sharply

Latin America is a region of great cultural contrasts. Contemporary "European" culture clashes with traditional people and lifestyles on the streets of many communities throughout the region.

divided socioeconomic classes, and other groups. Problems such as these can raise an insurmountable barrier to development in the affected countries. Only recently have portions of the region begun to experience a democratic tradition and the emergence of a well-educated, social middle class. Although rather spotty in distribution, a number of countries are beginning to experience stable economic growth and development. Most visitors to Latin America are shocked by the apparent lack of environmental awareness, concern, and ethics. This reality comes as a reminder that only an affluent society can afford the luxury of costly environmental safeguards. Today, however, there is growing concern for and attention given to protecting the environment.

Throughout Latin America, expectations are rising. In an increasingly global society, people are aware of what others have, and they want to share in the good fortune. The gap between the standard of living (desired goals) and scale of living (actual conditions) is great throughout much of the region, however. The disparity contributes to a widespread and, in many countries, a growing sense of restlessness, discontent, impatience, and frustration.

Racially, the region is a hodgepodge of peoples. Throughout much of the region, racial mixing has produced dominant populations of mixed ancestry. Culturally, very traditional societies—people living in much the same way they did centuries ago—can still be found in some remote areas. At the other extreme, Latin America is home to millions of people who are just as "contemporary" as is the typical Northern American. Other than for the language, an American or Canadian walking the streets of a typical Latin American city would feel quite "at home."

A REGION OF EXTREMES

In many respects, Latin America is a region of extremes. It is home to the world's driest desert and largest area of tropical wetlands. Parched lunar landscapes void of plant life stand in marked contrast to the vast tropical rain forest of the Amazon Basin. The Amazon is the world's greatest river by volume and Titicaca is the world's highest navigable lake. No place else on Earth can boast of having the world's highest, as well as its

Spectacular Lake Titicaca, which rises 12,500 feet (3,810 meters) above sea level on the border of Peru and Bolivia, is South America's second-largest lake and the world's highest lake navigable to large vessels.

widest and perhaps most spectacular, waterfalls. As a barrier, no mountain range is more formidable over as long a distance than the Andes. Some of history's greatest natural disasters also have occurred in Latin America. And Brazil receives more lightning strikes and records more lightning-caused deaths than any other country.

Latin America also exhibits many human extremes. Historically, it was home to several of the world's great early civilizations. Today, three of its cities rank among the world's ten largest. Brazil is home to more blacks and more Roman Catholics than any other country in the world. No country can come close to the record of political instability and often violent changes in government that has been established by Bolivia and Ecuador. Finally, three of the world's four top-ranking "murder capitals" are Latin American countries. On the other hand, several Latin American countries are models of political and social stability. Economically, the region is home to the world's largest dam, largest copper mine, largest ranch, and largest plantation. Haiti ranks at or near the bottom of all the world's countries in many indices of human well-being, corruption, poverty, and political instability. Mexico and Brazil, though, now rank among the world's top ten economic powers in terms of their gross domestic product.

As you begin your journey southward (actually, to the southeast!) into Latin America, it is important to keep several points in mind. First, the region is of great and rapidly growing importance to Northern Americans. Second, the region is unified by geographic location, history, and its dominant Iberian culture. Third, it is a region of great contrasts and extremes. Finally, it is impossible to stereotype a "typical" Latin American country or person. Welcome to Latin America . . . enjoy your trip!

CHAPTER 2

Diverse Natural Landscapes

Latin America is a region of great environmental contrasts and spectacular natural landscapes. In some places, nature has imposed huge obstacles to the development of transportation networks, human settlement, and economic development. In others, it has smiled kindly, offering an abundance of resources, opportunity, and good fortune. For thousands of years, each of the region's diverse environments has been "home" to some group of peoples. Some of the region's oldest archaeological sites—dating back thousands of years—are in cold and stormy southern Chile, the hot and humid Amazon Basin, and the parched desert coastal region of Peru.

CULTURE AND NATURE

The relationship that humans establish with the environment(s) in which they live is of great interest to geographers. Cultural ecology—the study of how people adapt to, use, and change the physical places in which they live—is one of geography's most fundamental and time-honored traditions. A century ago, some geographers believed that natural conditions strongly influenced (or even determined) the way people lived. For example, they spoke of "rain forest (or desert, or mountain) peoples" as if they were mere pawns of nature. Within each of Earth's ecosystems, tremendous cultural differences exist. Culture, not nature, influences how people live in and adapt to the natural environment. For example, in the deserts of northern Mexico live some of the Western Hemisphere's most traditional peoples. Several hundred miles distant, across the border in equally arid southern Arizona, are the modern bustling cities of Tucson and Phoenix. The humid tropical Amazon Basin is home to some of the world's most traditional tribal peoples. At the same time, one of the world's great cities, Rio de Janeiro, also shares this climatic condition.

Today, when studying cultural ecology, most geographers are interested in three important factors. First, they want to know how different cultures have adapted to the natural environment(s) in which they live. They ask questions such as, "Has nature been helpful, or has it hindered development and settlement?" and, "How have people adjusted to make living in a certain environment profitable and comfortable?"

Second, they want to know what natural resources are being used and how. A geographer might ask, "Why are some things used and others ignored?" "How are the resources being used?" "Is the current use of a resource that for which it is best suited?" The fragile Amazon rain forest ecosystem, for example, is being cleared at an alarming rate. People are flocking into the region in the hope of acquiring land to farm. The soils of the rain forest there are very infertile, however. Crop agriculture is

The world's second-longest river, the Amazon flows nearly 4,000 miles (6,437 kilometers) from the Andes Mountains in Peru to the Atlantic Ocean. Indigenous peoples are the primary inhabitants of the Amazon Basin, but the area remains mostly uninhabited.

not well suited to this environment. Ecotourism on the other hand, which would not destroy the natural setting and has great economic potential, is being largely ignored. Farming, mining, logging, fishing, or tourism based on scenery are examples of land and resource use.

Finally, geographers are interested in the ways human activities have changed natural environments. It also is important to recognize the consequences of such changes. Much of Latin America has been altered by human use. Forests have been and continue to be cleared. Land has been severely eroded. Waters have been polluted, as has the atmosphere over most Latin American cities. These are just a few examples of ways in which humans and nature have clashed.

In this chapter and several others, you will find many illustrations of the important relationship between culture and nature. Early Spaniards, for example, sought their fortunes in the gold- and silver-bearing ores of rugged mountainous areas. The Portuguese, on the other hand, were lured by the fertile, moist tropical coasts of Brazil, where sugarcane could thrive. At one time, the broad, fertile plain of the Argentine Pampas was the world's leading producer of agricultural export commodities. Today, as in the past, the natural environment plays a very important role in Latin America. As you will learn, it is a factor in accessibility, settlement, economic activity, and much more.

LANDFORM FEATURES

Imagine that you are in a spaceship high above the southern United States. The sky is cloudless, providing a wonderful view. To the southeast, you see a huge arc of islands. The closer ones—Cuba, Jamaica, Hispañola, and Puerto Rico—are large and rugged. These are the Greater Antilles, an archipelago (chain of islands) that separates the Caribbean Sea from the Gulf of Mexico. East of Puerto Rico, a chain of much smaller islands trails away to the southeast, then bends southward almost to the South American continent. These are the Lesser Antilles. Some of these islands are mountainous and others have low elevations and relatively flat terrain.

Looking south toward Mexico, you see what appears to be a high, rugged letter "Y" with its arms stretching toward the U.S. border. These are the Sierra Madre Oriental ("Mother Mountains of the East") and Sierra Madre Occidental ("Mother Mountains of the West"). Here and there, they are cut by deep gorges, some even larger than Arizona's Grand Canyon. Between the ranges is a high plateau that is home to most of Mexico's population. The Sierras join just south of Mexico City and continue southward, forming the backbone of southern Mexico and Central America. Sticking out like a "thumb" from southeastern Mexico is Yucatán. This flat, low-lying peninsula is the homeland of the Mayan people and the ruins of their once-great civilization. Today, it is perhaps better known for Cancún, one of the world's leading tourist destinations.

Drifting southeastward, you notice a huge landmass. You immediately recognize it as the 6.9-million-square-mile (17.9-million-square-kilometer) South American continent. You marvel at the panorama of diverse land features spread before you as far as you can see. Several features attract your attention. There is a huge, towering mountain range that extends the entire length of the continent along its western margin. Because higher peaks are snow covered throughout the entire 5,000-mile (8,000-kilometer) extent, you know the mountains are very high. You even see glacier- and snow-clad peaks on the equator! These are the Andes, the world's longest and second-highest mountain range. Over a stretch of about 3,500 miles (5,600 kilometers), peaks exceed 10,000 feet (3,000 meters). Northeast of Santiago, Chile, near the border with Argentina, a snow-capped peak towers over others in the area. It is the mighty Cerro Aconcagua, which soars to an elevation of 22,834 feet (6,960 meters), the highest point in the Western Hemisphere.

Looking southward and to the east of the Andes, the land features resemble a roller coaster of alternating highlands and lowlands. In Venezuela, the northern Andes bend eastward, dip beneath the Atlantic for a short distance, and then reemerge to form the nearby islands of Trinidad and Tobago. South of the Andes, the land becomes flat and almost featureless. This is the broad alluvial plain created by silt deposited by the Orinoco River.

South of the Orinoco, the terrain begins to rise abruptly. These are the Guiana Highlands, which extend across southern Venezuela and portions of the three Guianas (Guyana, Suriname, and French Guiana), and reach into northern Brazil. The highlands are home to a unique landform feature, the *tepui.* These mountains have nearly flat tops and are flanked by slopes that plunge almost vertically for thousands of feet. The highest

The Andes stretch some 3,500 miles (5,632 kilometers) from Venezuela in the north to Chile in the south. Inhabitants of the Andes often use the llama (pictured here) for its wool and to transport goods over the rugged terrain.

tabletop tepui is Mount Roraima (9,432 feet, or 2,876 meters), located near the point where Venezuela, Guyana, and Brazil meet. Roraima's flat top was the setting of Sir Arthur Conan Doyle's legendary 1912 book, *The Lost World*, which was made into a Hollywood movie in 1925.

The Guiana Highlands remain one of the world's most remote and inaccessible places. So little known is the region, in fact, that the world's highest waterfall was not discovered until 1935! In that year, American pilot Jimmy Angel spotted this spectacular cataract that bears his name from the air, through a break in the perpetual shield of clouds. Angel Falls begins with a straight plummet of 2,648 feet (807 meters), followed by a second fall of 564 feet (172 meters)—a total drop of 3,212 feet (979 meters).

Beyond the southern edge of the Guiana Highlands, the land dips downward again, into the Amazon Basin. This vast plain occupies an area as large as that of the United States west of the Mississippi River. Much of this area has never been seen from the ground, at least not by non-Amerindians. Here, almost without exception, travel is either by river or air. The dominant feature of the Amazon Basin is, of course, the giant river from which it takes its name (see box on page 18 for details). Within the basin, land rises on the *interfluves* (land between rivers). Most of the terrain is gently rolling. Bordering much of the Amazon, however, the floodplain is almost flat. In some places, the river's floodwaters can spread outward as many as 50 miles (80 kilometers). As you will learn later, there are many reasons why most of the Amazon Basin remains poorly developed, barely accessible, and sparsely populated.

South of the Amazon Basin, the land rises again. This is the upland region called the Brazilian Highlands, which occupies roughly the southern half of the country. Actually, it is misleading to think of this area as "mountains." More correctly, it is a tableland that slopes downward from east to west. Seen from the eastern coastal plain, the highlands form a formidable barrier as they rise from near sea level to nearly 9,500 feet (2,896 meters), just north of Rio de Janeiro. Atop the escarpment (steep slope), however, the rolling land slopes rather gently in a northward direction until it gradually flattens and disappears in the Amazon Basin.

Over millions of years, rivers have cut deep trenches in the highlands; these are ideal locations for dams. In many places, dams have been built to provide electricity for power-starved Brazil. On the southwestern edge of the Brazilian Highlands are two of the world's most incredible features—one man-made and the other natural.

AMAZON RIVER

- World's largest river in terms of volume, containing slightly more than 20 percent of all river flow.
- 4,000 miles (6,437 kilometers) long (about 100 miles [161 kilometers] shorter than longest river, the Nile).
- Drainage basin occupies about 2.7 million square miles (6.9 million square kilometers), or nearly 40 percent of the South American continent.
- Volume is four times greater than the Congo River, which has the second-greatest flow.
- Volume is 8.5 to 11 times greater than that of the Mississippi River.
- Source is Lake Lauricocha, in the Peruvian Andes; about 100 miles (161 kilometers) from the Pacific Ocean.
- 1,100 major tributaries with combined length of about 4 million miles (6.43 million kilometers).
- Seven tributaries more than 1,000 miles (1,610 kilometers) long.
- Navigable to oceangoing vessels to Iquitos, Peru (2,300 miles/3,700 kilometers).
- Varies in width from 1 to 35 miles (1.6 to 56 kilometers), and in many places land cannot be seen across the river.
- In 24 hours, average discharge is greater than the average U.S. daily rainfall.
- Each day, as much water discharged as New York City uses in nine years.
- Discharge of water creates a freshwater lens reaching up to 200 miles (320 kilometers) into the Atlantic.
- River is 150 to 200 miles (240 to 320 kilometers) wide at its mouth.
- River channel in Brazil has an average depth of 150 feet (46 meters), reaching 400 feet (122 meters) in places.
- River transports 1.3 million tons of sediment each day.
- The tidal bore (an upstream surge of water with rising tide in the Atlantic) creates a "wall" of water at river's mouth that can be 15 feet (4.6 meters) high and travel upstream 30 miles per hour (48 kilometers per hour).

Iguassú Falls cascades over the southern edge of the Brazilian Highlands. The majestic falls are nearly four times higher and five times as wide as Niagara Falls.

Itaipú Dam, on the Paraná River, is the world's largest. Built at a cost of $18.5 billion, the dam is 5 miles (8 kilometers) wide and 640 feet (195 meters) high. Not too far distant, near where Brazil, Paraguay, and Argentina meet, are the spectacular Iguassú Falls. With a width of 2.5 miles (4 kilometers), they are the world's widest falls. When the Iguassú River is in full flow, water cascades over as many as 275 cataracts with a maximum drop of 275 feet (84 meters).

Southward, the Brazilian Highlands give way to the lowland plains of the Paraná-Paraguay river system and the broad, fertile plains of the Argentine Pampas. In the north, much of the land is poorly drained marsh or swamp. In Uruguay and central Argentina, however, the flat land is ideal for ranching and crop agriculture. Finally, the continent begins to narrow as it reaches its southern tip, and the Patagonia Plateau is squeezed in between the Andes and the Atlantic Ocean. This rugged tableland is deeply cut by east-west flowing streams, making north–south travel difficult.

WEATHER

Atmospheric conditions—weather (current) and climate (long-term average)—is the single most important natural element. Vegetation, animal life habitat, and water features are largely determined by climate. Even landform features and soils are strongly affected by temperature and moisture. Certainly, human activity is keenly adapted to weather. Think of your home, clothing, and personal activities. How do you take advantage of, or protect against, weather conditions? Are there economic activities—such as growing (or not growing) certain crops, recreational activities, or tourism—for which weather and climate play an important role?

Most of Latin America lies within the tropical latitudes. Only the southern portion of the South American continent reaches into the temperate mid-latitudes. The region's position is of considerable geographical importance. Historically, tropical and subtropical lands did not attract mid-latitudes peoples. Europeans were not accustomed to the hot and either extremely wet or dry conditions. The cultural, economic, and social importance of this reality is discussed in greater depth in subsequent chapters.

Temperature

If "tropical" is defined as those areas located within 30 degrees latitude on each side of the equator, nearly 90 percent of Latin America is tropical. This definition, however, can be misleading. More correctly, "tropics" is defined by temperature. The average temperature of the coldest month must be above 65°F (18°C). Also, frost never occurs in tropical regions. Using this definition, some humid regions, such as the Amazon Basin, are tropical, but so are the hot desert regions of northern Mexico! Another characteristic of tropical regions is that weather is relatively constant. Because of their latitudinal location relatively near the equator, temperatures vary little from season to season.

Using latitude alone as a guideline for determining climate can be very misleading. Many other factors are involved. There are, after all, glaciers atop several high mountain peaks in Ecuador (named for the equator). Several controls in addition to latitude influence temperature. In much of Latin America, elevation is the most important control of temperature. As a general rule, temperatures decrease about 3.5°F with each 1,000-foot increase (6.5°C/1,000 meters) in elevation. Quito, Ecuador, is located just a few miles from the equator but at an elevation of 9,200 feet (2,800 meters). It experiences a chilly year-round temperature average of about 57°F (14°C). Only on rare occasions has the temperature reached above 80°F (27°C) or fallen below freezing. Manaus, Brazil, is also located near the equator, but at an elevation of only several hundred feet above sea level. Its year-round temperature averages 81°F (27°C). Maximum temperatures at this city in the heart of the Amazon have reached 100°F (38°C) but have only dropped into the mid-60s (about 18°C).

Temperatures are also influenced by a location's proximity to a large body of water. Places near an ocean will have a relatively small fluctuation in daily and annual temperatures. Inland, away from the moderating influence of the sea, temperatures will vary more widely. This is because land heats and cools faster and to greater extremes than does a body of water. In the northern interior of Mexico and Argentina, temperatures often soar above a scorching 100°F (38°C). During the cold season, however, they also can drop to 0°F (−18°C) or below, a seasonal range of more than 100°F (38°C). Locally, ocean currents also influence temperatures. Lima, Peru, for example, is located at 12 degrees south latitude but experiences monthly average temperatures ranging from the low 60s to low 70s

(16 to 21°C). The city is located just inland from the Pacific Ocean and its cold offshore Peru Current.

It may seem strange that the region's highest temperatures do not occur in the tropical latitudes. Rather, they are recorded in northern Mexico, near 30 degrees north latitude. This pattern can be explained by the distribution of atmospheric moisture (humidity) and cloud cover. In the equatorial latitudes, clouds serve as a shield, blocking incoming solar radiation (heat energy); temperatures rarely rise into the 90s (32°C). On the other hand, moisture in the atmosphere also serves as a blanket, holding in heat. So tropical temperatures are quite constant and never drop to extreme lows. In deserts, however, the atmosphere is relatively dry and cloudless. Temperatures here soar during the daytime and can become quite chilly at night.

Most of Latin America does not experience extremely cold temperatures. Culturally, for people accustomed to heat, high temperatures pose no problem, and in few places do temperatures drop to become life threatening. The author was once in the Amazon Basin when it experienced a near record low temperature—in the upper 50s (13 to 14°C). Local people were suffering greatly and many activities ceased because of the "extreme cold"!

Precipitation

Precipitation (any form of falling moisture) varies greatly from place to place and season to season throughout much of Latin America. Spatially, the area can be divided into three regions, each based on the amount and seasonal distribution of moisture it receives. As a general rule, within a belt extending about ten degrees on each side of the equator, heavy rains fall throughout the year. Most of this wet tropical area receives 60 to 80 inches (150 to 300 centimeters) a year, with some areas receiving as much as 300 inches (760 centimeters). At the opposite extreme, northwestern Mexico, coastal Peru and northern Chile, and much of Argentina's Patagonia Plateau

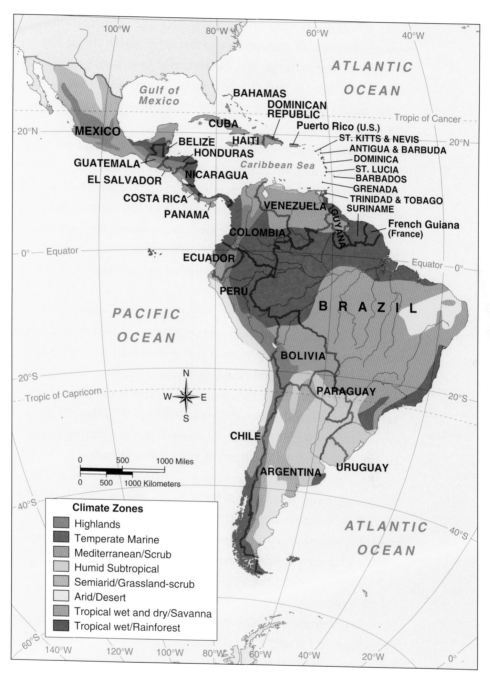

Climate Zones
- Highlands
- Temperate Marine
- Mediterranean/Scrub
- Humid Subtropical
- Semiarid/Grassland-scrub
- Arid/Desert
- Tropical wet and dry/Savanna
- Tropical wet/Rainforest

Much of Latin America's climate is considered tropical; however, much of north-western Mexico and portions of northern Chile and southern Peru are arid deserts.

are arid deserts. Less than 10 inches (25 centimeters) of precipitation falls each year, and in many places much less is received. Portions of northern Chile and southern Peru receive on average less than an inch (2 centimeters) of rain a year. Such places may go many years without receiving a drop of moisture!

Between these two extremes and making up much of Latin America is an area that experiences sharply divided wet and dry seasons. This region of tropical wet and dry climate receives an annual average of 40 to 60 inches (100 to 150 centimeters) of rainfall. Fully 90 percent of the rain occurs during the high-sun, or summer, season. The winter (low-sun) season is quite dry. Elsewhere in Latin America, precipitation falls at a level between these extremes.

Throughout Latin American, as elsewhere, some human activities are adapted to moisture conditions. Whether very wet or extremely dry, people have learned to survive and often thrive. There are several problem areas, however. In northern Mexico, in recent decades, population has grown and both agriculture and industry have expanded greatly. Here, the lack of moisture is beginning to place severe limits on future growth. In the area of northeastern Brazil that protrudes into the Atlantic, moisture is unpredictable. During normal years, the region receives 10 to 40 inches (25 to 100 centimeters) of rainfall, but severe droughts are frequent. During dry years, crops fail, streams dry up, pasturelands wither, and the region's people, chronically Brazil's poorest, suffer even more.

Wind Systems

Some weather patterns in Latin America can only be explained by global wind systems. The patterns are quite simple. In both hemispheres from about 30 to 60 degrees, winds generally blow from the west; these are the prevailing westerlies. From the equator to about 30 degrees north latitude, winds blow from the northeast as the northeast trade winds. At comparable latitudes in the Southern Hemisphere, they blow from the southeast as the southeast trade winds.

A precipitation map will show that southern Chile receives more than 80 inches (200 centimeters) of precipitation a year. Yet at the same latitude, east of the Andes in Argentina, precipitation drops to below 10 inches (25 centimeters). Here, the prevailing westerlies drop their moisture on the windward- (western-) facing slopes of the Andes. As the winds descend onto the Patagonia Plateau, they have little moisture left, thereby creating desert conditions. Travelers to the Caribbean will find lush wet tropical conditions on the northern part of mountainous islands such as Jamaica or Puerto Rico. They may be shocked, however, to find near-desert conditions along the southern coasts. The northeast trade winds drop most of their moisture on the northern slopes and coastal plains, which leaves little precipitation for the interior highlands.

El Niño

In recent decades, scientists have realized that a change in water temperature off the coast of Peru and Ecuador is responsible for many global weather events. Every few years, the normally cold water of the Peru Current is replaced by the warm water of the tropical Pacific. This phenomenon is called *El Niño* (named for the Christ child, because it often appears during the Christmas season). When an El Niño occurs, it brings drought to some areas and floods to others. Some locations experience much higher temperatures, whereas others shiver in below-normal temperatures, and there is an increase in storm frequency and intensity in many places.

CLIMATES AND ECOSYSTEMS

Climate is the primary factor in the formation of ecosystems—those closely interrelated complexes that include vegetation, animal life, and soil. Each ecosystem also offers potential and perhaps presents problems for human development.

Tropical Rain Forests

A tropical wet climate and tropical rain forest ecosystem extends throughout much of equatorial South America. It also extends along the southeast coast of Brazil, the eastern margins of Central America, and the northern portions of mountainous Caribbean islands. This ecosystem is dominated by huge amounts of precipitation, most of which falls during often violent thundershowers. Temperatures are hot and sultry year-round, with humidity always high. It is, in fact, a very monotonous climate. Annual monthly averages vary by only a few degrees, and seldom will a daytime-to-nighttime temperature span be more than 20°F (7°C). "Nighttime," it is often said, "is the winter of the tropics."

With the constant heat and moisture, vegetation thrives. This area is home to the tropical rain forest, the world's richest and most diverse ecosystem. As trees reach upward, they form a thick overhead canopy that blocks sunlight from reaching the forest floor, where very little plant life grows. Some trees grow to heights of 200 feet (60 meters). No place in the world can match the rain forest for the diversity of vegetation. As many as 400 different tree species can be found within a small area. Tens of thousands of vines, creepers, mosses, ferns, and other plants crowd the forest landscape. One commonly held belief about rain forests is that they are "jungles." *Jungle* refers to a very dense, almost impenetrable growth of vegetation. As mentioned previously, because of the thick overhead canopy, the floor of tropical rain forests are relatively clear of plant growth. Jungle is found only where sunlight reaches the forest floor, such as along roads, railroads, rivers, or clearings. These "jungle" environments, of course, are the kinds of places most visitors to the tropics experience. As a result, the myth that all rain forest is jungle continues to be widely believed.

Animal life, too, is incredibly diverse. In fact, the rain forest ecosystem is home to 80 percent of all plant and animal species.

The tapir is the largest wild animal that lives in the tropical rain forest. Three species of these piglike herbivores inhabit Latin America, including this Brazilian, or lowland tapir.

Surprisingly, perhaps, there are very few large animals in the rain forest. The largest is the manatee, an aquatic animal that may grow to a length of 15 feet (5 meters) and weigh up to one ton. On land, the tapir is the largest wild animal. This strange-looking herbivore has been described as "a pig that started out as an elephant, then decided it wanted to be a horse, then changed its mind again."

Because their flesh is highly prized for consumption by humans, both the manatee and tapir are threatened with extinction. Larger animals include many kinds of rodents, giant anteaters, jaguars, and ocelots. There are also many kinds of monkeys, including the howler, which emits the loudest animal sound in nature, sounding much like a jet plane!

Birds and insects abound in the rain forest, as do various reptiles. Many insects, including flies, mosquitoes, and sand flies, transmit diseases, some of which are deadly. Snakes include the venomous fer-de-lance, coral, and bushmaster, all of which can be deadly. The water boa, or anaconda, is a constrictor and also the world's largest snake, reaching a length of more than 30 feet (10 meters). Tropical waters teem with fish, including hundreds of edible species on which local populations depend as a chief source of food. One of the best-known fish is the razor-sharp-toothed piranha. These small, bluegill-sized predators travel in schools. They can kill and strip the flesh from a large animal in minutes.

Traditionally, the rain forest was inhabited by tribal peoples who hunted, fished, and gathered for their livelihood. Today, these people are in decline. A primitive form of shifting cultivation is practiced in many tropical areas. Most tropical soils are quite poor, so farm plots produce low yields and must be moved every few years. This contributes to deforestation, a major threat to this extremely important, yet very fragile, ecosystem.

Tropical Savanna

In the region of seasonally wet and dry tropical conditions, the woodlands of the wet tropics give way to tropical savannas. Here, tall grasses thrive together with a few scattered fire-resistant trees. Scientists believe that the savanna ecosystem is artificial; that is, it is created by human activity. During the wet season, vegetation grows profusely, but when conditions dry out, so do the plants. As a result, for thousands of years, residents have used fire to clear the land of the dried, useless vegetation. Through time, this has favored grasslands and a few trees that are resistant to flames. It has created an open, parkland environment. Livestock grazing is the major land use in this region. Huge herds of cattle thrive on the Llanos grasslands of the Orinoco Basin and the Campos of the Brazilian Highlands.

Grassland-Scrub

In areas receiving between about 10 and 30 inches (25 to 75 centimeters) of precipitation, savanna gives way to a grassland-scrubland vegetation that varies depending on local conditions. Here, soils are more fertile, but rainfall is unreliable. Subsistence farming and livestock grazing are major economic activities.

Desert

The arid desert ecosystem is found in those places receiving less than 10 inches (25 centimeters) of moisture a year. In some places, as in northern Chile's Atacama Desert, vegetation and animal life are all but absent. This is the world's driest place. Years have passed with not a drop of rain. Northern Mexico and Argentina's Patagonia Plateau also have an arid climate and desert landscape.

Plants are small and scattered and must adapt in some way to the condition of aridity and torrid summer temperatures. Some have very deep root systems that can reach far down to soil moisture. Many plants have small leaves to reduce water loss through transpiration. Water is the key to desert survival. At oasis sites (places where fresh water is available), irrigated agriculture and other human activities are possible.

Mid-Latitude Climates and Ecosystems

Only the southern part of South America reaches into the middle latitudes. Here, temperatures are somewhat cooler, and weather is marked by four distinct seasons. Because of these more moderate conditions, the areas attracted millions of European settlers. As a result, much of the natural vegetation rapidly gave way to agriculture. Crops replaced the original plant life in much of the region and Old World–introduced livestock replaced native wild herbivores. There are three distinct climates and ecosystems.

A humid subtropical climate spreads across the Argentine Pampas and into Uruguay, the southern tip of Brazil, and southern Paraguay. This is Latin America's most agriculturally productive area. Conditions are very similar to those of the southeastern United States. Rainfall is plentiful, and the growing season is long. Soils are fertile.

Central Chile enjoys what many people consider to be the world's most ideal climate—the Mediterranean. This climate, which also is found in southern coastal California, is mild and pleasant. It is unique in that the Mediterranean is the only climate that experiences a pronounced summer drought. Precipitation is ample, but nearly all of it falls as winter rain. Because of the long period of drought, vegetation dries out, resulting in a severe fire threat during the summer months. Here, as in the savannas, vegetation must be able to survive frequent burning, resulting in a scrubland condition. In most of the region, however, the original natural vegetation was replaced long ago by crop- and pastureland.

Southern Chile has a temperate marine climate, similar to that of coastal northern California northward to the Alaskan panhandle. Because of its proximity to the ocean, temperatures are not extreme. This area receives high amounts of precipitation, though, with some areas recording up to a drenching 300 inches (760 centimeters). Few people live in this area, and because of frequent storms and very rugged terrain, there is little logging of the region's forests.

ENVIRONMENTAL HAZARDS

Latin America experiences numerous natural hazards, many of which can be deadly and devastating. From deep within the earth come violent earthquakes and powerful volcanic eruptions. Each year, treacherous hurricanes sweep through the Caribbean Sea and Gulf of Mexico, ravaging everything within their path. Low-lying settlements along the Pacific coast face the threat of being inundated by a tsunami. Those on the

Atlantic side can be destroyed by the surge of water pushed on land by tropical storms. Many places are subject to occasional droughts and others to periodic river or lowland flooding. Rock avalanches, mudflows, and other gravity-caused hazards often devastate property and take the lives of people living below.

The following list of major natural disasters must be read with caution. Many of these events occurred in remote areas and in countries too poor to keep detailed records. Deaths and property damage (where listed) are little more than estimates. Keep in mind that these are only major events. When added together, the toll of these natural events—on lives, property, and other losses—is indeed staggering.

MAJOR NATURAL DISASTERS

1780—**Hurricane** sweeps through the Lesser Antilles, killing an estimated 22,000 people (the deadliest hurricane on record).

1877—**Eruption** of Mount Cotopaxi in north-central Ecuador causes mudflows that destroy a number of communities and results in 1,000 deaths.

1902—**Eruption** of Mount Pelée on Martinique, in the Lesser Antilles, destroys the city of St. Pierre, killing 40,000.

1930—**Hurricane** strikes Dominican Republic, killing 8,000.

1939—**Earthquake** in central Chile damages 50,000 square miles (130,000 square kilometers) and kills 30,000.

1960—**Earthquake** measuring 9.5 on the Richter scale (the highest ever recorded) hits near Chile's south-central coast, killing 2,000.

1962—**Avalanche** down Mount Huascaran buries villages and takes 3,000 lives.

1970—**Earthquake** in Peru takes 67,000 lives.

1972—**Earthquake** devastates Managua, Nicaragua, leaving 6,000 dead.

1974—**Hurricane** strikes Honduras, leaving 100,000 homeless and 8,000 dead.

1976—**Earthquake** destroys Guatemala City, Guatemala, leaving an estimated 25,000 dead and one-sixth of the country's population homeless.

1985—**Eruption** of Colombia's Nevado del Ruiz creates mudslides that bury several towns and leave 25,000 dead.

1997—**Eruption** of Soufriere Hills volcano on Montserrat, in the Lesser Antilles, ongoing since 1995, leaves southern two-thirds of the island uninhabitable, forces 8,000 of the island's 12,000 residents to flee, and takes 20 lives.

1998—**Hurricane** "Mitch" strikes Guatemala, Honduras, and Nicaragua, leaving up to 3 million people homeless, more than 11,000 dead, and $5 billion in damage.

1999—**Earthquake** in west-central Colombia leaves 200,000 homeless and kills 1,200.

1999—**Flooding and mudslides** in northern Venezuela, in and around Caracas, leave a half-million people homeless, cause billions of dollars in property losses, and kills up to 15,000.

2001—**Earthquake** in El Salvador sets off nearly 200 **mudslides**, destroying 100,000 houses and leaving nearly 1,000 dead.

In the following chapters, you will learn much more about the role nature plays in Latin America's patterns of settlement, economy, and many other aspects of the region's geographic conditions.

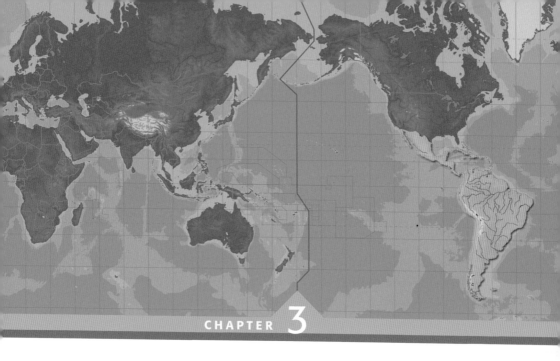

CHAPTER 3

Native Cultures

Geographers and others who seek to understand the present or forecast the future must first look to the past. Without knowing something about Latin America's historical geography, it is all but impossible to grasp contemporary conditions and patterns.

Today, large areas of the region remain predominantly Amerindian in both race and culture. Where did these first Americans come from, when did they arrive, and how did they get here? What were the early native cultures like? What was the impact of European exploration, settlement, and exploitation? Why did the Portuguese settle in Brazil and Spaniards throughout most of the remainder of Latin America? Why is the majority population in much of tropical Latin

America African in origin? These and other questions will be answered in this chapter, which focuses on Latin America's fascinating and often turbulent historical geography.

THE FIRST AMERICANS

The first Americans came from elsewhere. Several decades ago, archaeologists believed they knew who these early people were and where they came from. Scientists also thought they knew the route by which they traveled to this new land and when they arrived. Asian peoples, most believed, followed large game animals across Beringia (the Bering Strait "Land Bridge," or land exposed when sea level dropped during the Ice Age). They then passed through an ice-free corridor located between two huge masses of glacial ice that covered much of northern North America. Finally, they reached what is now the southwestern United States some 12,000 to 13,000 years ago.

Today, considerable doubt is being cast on this hypothesis. In fact, the origin of the first Americans is emerging as one of the great unanswered human "mysteries" of our time. And much archaeological evidence leading to the present state of confusion comes from Latin America. Some scientists now believe that rather than a single origin and group, America's earliest settlers came from many areas and at various times. Southeast Asia, Japan, and eastern Siberia have all been suggested as the source area(s), but so have Europe, Africa, and even Australia. Many scientists now believe that the Beringia route leading to the ice-free corridor would have been far too cold and inhospitable for travel; some even doubt that an ice-free corridor ever existed.

Perhaps the most convincing evidence comes from archaeological sites scattered throughout Latin America. The oldest widely agreed upon archaeological sites in the United States and Canada date back perhaps 13,000 to 20,000 years. Logically, if the earliest peoples came from the north, that is where the most ancient evidence should be found. But this is not the case. In fact, just the opposite is true. Currently, the oldest generally accepted evidence of human habitation is the Monte Verde site, located in southern Chile and dated to perhaps 33,000 years ago! The Pedra Furada site in eastern Brazil has been dated to 30,000 YBP (years before present), and what appear to be human footprints discovered recently in Mexico have been dated back 40,000 years. Some archaeologists, of course, question the accuracy of these dates. But it seems quite likely that humans have lived in Latin America for a very long time.

Support is gaining for a migration by which early peoples followed a coastal route and perhaps even traveled by water during part (or even all) of their journey. During the Ice Age, sea level was several hundred feet lower than it is now. Coastal land now under water would have been above sea level—a natural corridor for human migration.

Perhaps the full story of the earliest Americans will never be known. In fact, the question is much more academic than practical in nature. Almost certainly, pre-European arrivals represented a variety of human physical types, including Mongoloid, Negroid, and Caucasoid. This suggests multiple migrations and from different source areas, which almost certainly was the case. And such migrations may have occurred by both land and water over a time span of thousands of years.

A PROUD NATIVE HERITAGE

When Europeans first reached the Americas about 500 years ago, they found a huge continental island inhabited by an estimated 50 to 60 million native peoples. (Estimates range from a low of 8 million to a high of 112 million.) The figure itself is not that important. What is significant is that by all estimates, 90 to 95 percent of all early Americans lived in what is now Latin America. And there is little doubt that the great majority of them were concentrated into two relatively small areas: central and southern Mexico and the Central Andean area.

Levels of cultural development in Latin America varied greatly. In some of the more remote areas, people practiced a very

Located in south-central Peru, Machu Picchu reflects the level of cultural development the Incas achieved prior to European conquest. The ancient town is made up of several hundred stonework buildings, huge terraces, and other structures.

traditional culture, living as did much of humankind thousands of years ago. Elsewhere, groups such as the Maya and Aztec of Mexico and Inca of the central Andes achieved levels of cultural development comparable (and in some cases superior!) to that of Western Europe at the time of the conquest. The following discussion of preconquest cultures divides Latin America's native peoples on the basis of their economic activity.

Hunting-Fishing-Gathering Peoples

Originally, all Amerindians hunted and gathered for their livelihood. Those living by water also fished. A very small number of these people exist even today in some of the more remote and inaccessible areas of wet tropical South America. With the possible exception of some fisher folk, most such people were seminomadic. They moved from place to place so as not to deplete the game or food plants in one place. Populations were small and material possessions were few. Even today, the few people still practicing this way of life can generally pick up and carry all of their possessions.

Several groups warrant special mention. Tribes living at the far southern tip of South America were among the world's most isolated, and therefore primitive, peoples. Despite the extremely harsh (cold and stormy) environment, they subsisted on marine resources. Women dived into the frigid water to gather shellfish, which was their main source of food. Their housing consisted of crude brush huts, and they had little clothing, wearing only shawls. Even more amazing, they were one of the few groups in the world who did not know how to create fire—they were fire keepers. When Magellan passed through the strait that bears his name, he noticed many (of the kept) fires burning, hence the region's name, *Tierra del Fuego* ("Land of Fire"). A number of different tribal groups living in the Brazilian Highlands hunted game and gathered wild foods such as seeds, fruits and nuts, honey, locusts, and bird eggs.

Specialized Hunters

People living on the Pampas and southward on the Patagonia Plateau were specialized hunters. They used fire to hunt the guanaco (wild llama-like animal) and rhea (a large bird, like the ostrich, that runs rather than flies), thus creating the famous grasslands of the Pampas. These hunters also developed and used one of the world's most unique hunting devices, *bolas*. After the arrival of the Spaniards (and horses), these hunters became the famed *gauchos* (cowboys) of the Pampas region.

Simple Farmers

Simple farming peoples inhabited much of Latin America's tropical lowlands. They practiced a primitive form of slash-burn, subsistence, and shifting cultivation. Vegetation was slashed, allowed to dry, and burned. Tools were limited to knives, pointed digging sticks, and in some areas the hoe. Crops were planted in a scattered fashion and were barely if ever tilled. They included the root crop manioc, sweet potatoes, peanuts, pineapple, and hot peppers. Yields were meager, providing only enough food for the planter and her family. Because the tropical soils are heavily leached, they became infertile after several years. As a result, fields were eventually abandoned as the family or small village shifted to a new location. Women were engaged in agriculture; men continued to hunt or fish to provide protein for their family.

Among these Latin American tribes were the Jívaro, Carib, and Araucanian. The Jívaros live in the rain forest of eastern Ecuador. They were the only headhunters in the Americas. Heads were taken from killed enemies. Skin was removed from the skull and repeatedly filled with hot sand until it dried and shrunk to fist size. The skin was then treated with preservatives from plant extracts, and the lips of the shrunken skull were sewn shut. Needless to say, this practice is no longer continued! Another group, the Caribs, lived in northeastern South America. Their name comes from a grizzly practice observed by the earliest Spaniards in the region: cannibalism. *Carib* comes from the Spanish *caribal*, meaning "cannibal." Now you know the meaning of the Caribbean (cannibal) Sea!

Advanced Farmers of the Central Andes

Productive agriculture was the root of most early civilizations. Latin America was no exception. Here, early peoples domesticated and cultivated a number of crops and several animals. From Mesoamerica (Mexico and Central America) came maize (corn), several varieties of beans, squash, hot peppers, and cotton. These crops, and others, provided the foundation for the mighty Olmec, Mayan, and Aztec civilizations. To the south, in the northern and central Andean area, potatoes, sweet potatoes, peanuts, and manioc were added to the list of cultivated plants. Llamas and their smaller relative, the alpaca, were domesticated, as were guinea pigs. Here, the Incan culture developed and thrived among primarily Quechua-speaking peoples.

Archaeologists believe that the earliest civilizations in the Americas were those of the central Andean area in present-day Peru. Here, cultures were based on coastal fishing and inland-river-valley-irrigated agriculture. With an adequate food supply, populations began to grow and people began to specialize. Highly stratified societies developed. The discovery of ancient temples and pyramids suggests that the settlements were ruled by religious leaders. At the bottom, no doubt, were common laborers. In between were people involved in various activities that required specific skills. Inland farming peoples grew not only such food crops as sweet potatoes, beans, and squash but also cotton. From the cotton, skilled weavers made nets that were traded to coastal fisherfolk in exchange for fish and shellfish. In this way, the two quite different societies thrived in this otherwise harsh desert environment. Excavations suggest that Caral, an ancient ruin located near the coast north of Lima, may be the oldest city in the Americas and one of the world's oldest. It began to flourish around 3000 B.C., making the city nearly 1,000 years older than the earliest urban centers in Mexico.

Moche and Chimú

Peru was home to several important early cultures. In the north, the Moche culture thrived from about A.D. 200 to 800. It was followed by the Chimú Empire, which flourished from about A.D. 1000 to 1470. Both peoples also depended on irrigated agriculture and coastal fishing. There is also evidence that they practiced widespread trade, by land and by sea. The Chimú capital, Chan Chan, may have been the largest city in pre-European South America. It is believed to have had a population of 50,000 people, who occupied up to 10,000 adobe (earth brick) homes.

Nazca

Southern coastal Peru is home to one of the world's great mysteries. Here, more than 1,500 years ago, Nazca (also *Nasca*) people etched more than 300 figures into the desert surface. These "Nazca Lines," as they are called, occupy an area of nearly 400 square miles (1,040 square kilometers), forming the world's greatest concentration of earth art. Features vary from straight lines and geometric patterns to designs showing birds, humans, plants, and animals. Why they were created remains a mystery.

The Inca Empire

By A.D. 1200, Peru had experienced 4,000 years of extraordinary cultural development. The region, by nearly any measure, had become one of the world's major "culture hearths." From these roots sprang what was to become one of the world's most advanced cultures and civilizations, the Inca Empire. Here, however, a distinction must be made between the *culture* of Quechua-speaking people, which evolved over thousands of years, and the much shorter period of Incan *rule*. The first Incan (ruler) came to power in 1438, and the empire was conquered by Spain's Francisco Pizarro in 1533, having lasted less than a century.

From its capital in Cuzco, Peru, the empire rapidly spread northward to Ecuador and southward to central Argentina and Chile. Expansion was primarily cultural rather than by military force. "Conquered" people recognized that there were many advantages to being Inca. They eagerly accepted Quechua as their language and adopted political, social, and economic ways of Incan living. At its peak, the Inca Empire may have had a population of 37 million, with perhaps 5 to 6 million people living in its central Andean core area. This amazingly high population was supported by very productive agriculture. Potatoes were the primary food crop, although the Incas raised a variety of grains, fruits, and vegetables. Domesticated llamas provided meat and wool, and also served as beasts of burden, carrying packs weighing up to 80 pounds (36 kilograms). Steep mountainsides were terraced, water was diverted (often over distances of many miles) for irrigation, and guano (excrement of seafowl) was used as fertilizer.

The Incas also were skilled builders. Their roadways and water diversion systems rivaled those of Europeans at the time. Engineers marvel at their mountainside agricultural terracing, irrigation systems, and suspension bridges. Their stonework was superior to that of the Spaniards—even though the Incas lacked metal tools! Sacsayhuaman, the huge stone fortress built to protect Cuzco, is said by some military historians to have been the world's finest fortress.

One of the world's best known and most highly treasured ruins is Machu Picchu. This spectacular, long-abandoned Incan city is perched on a mountainside northwest of Cuzco. Several hundred stonework buildings, huge terraces, and other structures are spead over a 5-square-mile (13-square-kilometer) area. The site is at an elevation of about 8,000 feet (2,440 meters), sitting precariously 2,000 feet (610 meters) above the rushing Urubamba River. Although there are many theories, no one knows why Machu Picchu was built (sometime around A.D. 1400). Perhaps it fulfilled some unknown ceremonial function, or may have been the Incas' vacation retreat.

Despite its size, the ruins cannot be seen from the valley floor. Amazingly, Spaniards never knew the ruins existed! It was not until 1911—four centuries after the Spanish conquest—that Machu Picchu was rediscovered. An American, Hiram Bingham, was leading an expedition down the Urubamba Valley in search of archaeological sites. One day, they met a young boy who offered (for a dime) to show them some ruins. Can you imagine their surprise when, after the long climb up the mountainside, they stumbled upon one of the world's most spectacular archaeological treasures!

Mesoamerican Civilizations

Early civilizations also flourished in central and eastern Mexico from about 1500 B.C. until the Spanish conquest. Here, as in the central Andes, they built upon earlier contributions by many cultures that had existed in the region for several millennia. Earlier peoples had developed productive agricultural systems, producing huge yields of maize, beans, squash, and other crops. A reliable food supply supported rapid population growth and urbanization. Freed from the task of food production, many people became specialized craftsmen. They made pots, jewelry, or woven fabrics that could be exchanged for other items. In this way, some cities grew as market centers supported by widespread trade. Others, judging from their huge and often elaborate pyramids and temples, were primarily ceremonial centers.

Olmec

One early civilization, the Olmec, occupied the coastal lowlands bordering the Gulf of Mexico immediately to the west of the Yucatán Peninsula. They were a highly creative people whose culture began to appear around 1500 B.C. and continued a century or two into the Christian era. Olmecs were among the first people in the Americas to make pottery and perhaps the first to develop a simple written language. They built the first pyramids in the Americas, huge structures with a mass comparable to those of Egypt, and their stone architecture was superb. As artists, they made beautiful jewelry and were skilled painters and sculptors.

The Olmecs are best remembered for three contributions. First, they had a part in one of archaeology's great mysteries: the construction of many huge stone heads weighing up to 10 tons. Researchers have been unable to determine why they were made. Second, the Olmecs were the only peoples of the New World to have created the wheel. Rather than putting it to use for transportation purposes, however, the Olmecs used it only to make toys. Why the wheel, certainly one of humankind's most useful inventions, was not used for work also remains a mystery. Finally, it is believed that the Olmecs were the first to domesticate the cacao tree, the source of chocolate. So if you enjoy chocolate as a drink, cake, candy, or ice cream flavor, you have the ancient Olmecs to thank!

Mayan

To the east, in what is now Belize and portions of Guatemala and on the Yucatán Peninsula, another high culture emerged around 1100 B.C.—the Mayan. These creative people developed what is now recognized as having been the most advanced culture in Mesoamerica. Today, thousands of tourists flock to ancient Mayan ruins—cities, pyramids, ceremonial centers, and many other marvelous stone-built structures. Evidence exists that Mayans were also skilled in making accurate astronomical observations. Their written language and mathematical skills were the most advanced in the Americas.

Sometime around A.D. 900, for unknown reasons, Mayan cities were abandoned and their civilization mysteriously vanished. Scientists continue to search for an explanation of the Mayan decline. Could it have resulted from drought, disease, soil erosion, or some other natural cause? Or might overpopulation, social chaos, or warfare have contributed? Today, millions of Mayan-speaking people live in the region; it was the high civilization, not the Mayan people, that died out.

Teotihuacán

Yet another great archaeological mystery is tucked away in the Valley of Mexico, just a short distance northeast of Mexico City. Here were found the vast ruins of Teotihuacán. Between A.D. 200 and 600, the city's population swelled to an estimated 125,000 to 200,000 people, making it the largest urban center in the Americas and perhaps the world at the time. The city was both a center of manufacturing and trade. It lay astride major trade routes and goods made here have been found in archaeological sites throughout Mesoamerica. Teotihuacán also functioned as a major ceremonial center. The city's 180-foot- (55-meter-) high Pyramid of the Sun is the world's largest in area, with a base bigger than even Egypt's greatest pyramid.

Teotihuacán is shrouded in mystery. Why the city was built and by whom is unknown. Nothing is known of the city's

At its height, between A.D. 200 and 600, the Mexican city of Teotihuacán had between 125,000 and 200,000 inhabitants. The city not only served as a hub for trade and manufacturing but was also an important spiritual center for one of the earliest Mesoamerican civilizations.

government, and no tombs or statues of rulers have been found. No one knows why (or how!) the people built two huge pyramids. Despite living in an area of constant conflict, they appear to have lived peacefully. No evidence has been unearthed of soldiers, weapons, fortifications, or warfare. The greatest mystery, however, is their disappearance. Suddenly, late in the seventh century, the people and their culture disappeared and the city withered away.

Aztec

By the early fourteenth century, Mexico's earlier high civilizations had vanished. Into this cultural vacuum came a group of people from northern Mexico, the Mexica, later called the Aztecs. They settled in the Valley of Mexico, an area that at the time was home to many warring tribes. Seeking protection from hostilities, they built a city—Tenochtitlán—on an island in Lake Texcoco. (The lake was drained in the 1600s, and the former lake bottom is now the site of Mexico City). From this small urban refuge, the Aztecs eventually carved out the largest empire Mesoamerica had ever known. At its peak, some 30 million people were under their control. (Europe's largest country at the time had a population of about 20 million.)

Tenochtitlán, the Aztec capital, was a huge, spectacular, and in many ways unique city. It was built on a foundation of mud dredged from the bottom of Lake Texcoco. Bridges and causeways linked the city with the lake's shore. Within the city itself, people traveled from place to place on tree-lined canals. Farmland was created by building islands in the shallow lake. These islands, called *chinampas*, proved to be some of the world's most fertile farmland, producing huge yields of maize, beans, squash, and other staple foods.

The Aztecs grew to become a major military power, capable of conquering the region's other tribal groups and spreading their empire. Conquered peoples were forced to pay tribute to the Aztecs. Gold and other precious items, various tropical products from the coastal lowlands, foods, woven goods, and other commodities flowed into Tenochtitlán from throughout the empire. Tribute also included humans, most of whom were captured prisoners who faced a horrible fate—sacrifice to the Aztec gods. The Aztecs believed that their gods had given their own blood to create human life. By giving the gift of human life in return, they believed they could keep their gods content. On one occasion, this bloody practice reportedly led to the sacrifice of 20,000 captured prisoners in a single day! Victims were taken to the top of a temple pyramid and placed on an altar. While their arms and legs were held, a priest using a razor-sharp knife made of obsidian (volcanic glass) ripped open the victim's chest. The heart, still beating, was plucked from the body and held high by the priest as an offering to the gods. This brutal practice lasted for more than a century.

In addition to their building skills, powerful military and organizational capability, and brutal religious practices, the Aztecs developed a number of other noteworthy traits. They created a solar calendar with 365 days that was comparable in its precision to the calendar we use today. Much is known about Aztec history because they developed a written language and kept detailed written records. Aztec youngsters attended school. They received instruction about their history and culture and also many practical skills. Boys received military training and also learned about agriculture and other trades.

By 1520, the Aztecs faced growing unrest. Their neighbors were tired of paying tribute and having their people sacrificed. Things were changing, and change was unsettling, but the Aztecs had no idea what they were about to encounter! According to legend, Quetzalcoátl, a light-skinned, powerful priest, had once visited the Aztec homeland from some place far across the sea. Quetzalcoátl, it is said, violently opposed human sacrifices, a stand that made him unpopular among the Aztec rulers. In disgust of the continuing practice, Quetzalcoátl returned to the coast and sailed eastward into the Atlantic. As he departed, he promised to return in the year One Reed (an event that occurs every 52 years) in the Aztec calendar. The Aztecs believed that in this year of dread and disaster, the world could end. Little could they know that in that year and far across the Atlantic, a Spanish adventurer named Hernán Cortés was about to set sail for Mexico. Much of the Quetzalcoátl myth would soon become reality!

CHAPTER 4

European Heritage

It is highly probable that adventurers from the Old World reached the Americas on numerous occasions long before Columbus's voyage. Historically, however, Columbus's October 12, 1492, landfall on San Salvador (Watling), a small island in the eastern Bahamas, marks the beginning of what geographers call the New World Revolution. His arrival set in motion a series of events leading to the greatest demographic (population) and cultural revolution the world has ever experienced. Over a period of several centuries, Old World peoples and their culture would conquer and largely replace native peoples and their ways of life.

EARLY EXPLORATION AND SETTLEMENT

During the fourteenth century, Iberians—Spanish and Portuguese—had become a powerful seafaring force. Much of their success can be attributed to Prince Henry, "The Navigator," of Portugal. During the early 1400s, he established a school of navigation that brought about many improvements in shipbuilding, sails, and navigation. Christopher Columbus, sailing for the Spanish Crown, was but the first of many Iberian navigators to sail westward across the Atlantic. Some came in search of a route to the riches of the Orient; others sought new lands and wealth.

Did Worms Play a Role in the Naming of America?

On his fourth voyage to the Americas in 1502, Columbus found his ships' wooden hulls "badly worm eaten . . . and leaking alarmingly." The damage had been inflicted by a marine borer common to Caribbean waters, the teredo worm. Columbus was forced to put ashore for 11 days. Although the specific location remains in doubt, some geographers and historians now believe that it was along the Atlantic coast of Nicaragua.

Many historians suggest that America was named after the explorer Amerigo Vespucci. But there is another intriguing theory. Along what is now believed to have been the Nicaraguan coast, Columbus and his crewmen found Indians adorned in gold jewelry and ornaments. It would be quite natural for them to ask where the gold came from and, logically, the natives would have pointed inland to the source—the Amerrique Mountains! Might this have been the origin of the name *America* that in 1507 appeared on a map drafted by Martin Waldseemüller?

Spain Secures a Foothold

Columbus first established a small settlement on the north coast of the Caribbean island of Hispañola. Finding the site unsatisfactory, the settlement was abandoned in 1496 and moved to the island's south coast. The new community was named Santo Domingo by the Spaniards. The city, now the bustling capital of the Dominican Republic, thus became the first permanent European settlement in the New World. It also became the "nerve center" for the Spaniards' New World operations. Spain's New World interest focused primarily on finding gold and other mineral wealth. By 1511, Cuba, Puerto Rico, Jamaica, and Trinidad had been explored and colonized. Not surprisingly, these are the Caribbean islands on which gold was found.

CONQUEST AND THE SPREAD OF A SPANISH EMPIRE

By the early 1520s, Spanish influence had spread to the mainland coasts of present-day Mexico, Panama, Colombia, and Venezuela. Within two decades, the Spanish had conquered and colonized much of what is today Spanish Latin America. In 1519, Hernán Cortés and a band of 600 soldiers and sailors landed on Mexico's Caribbean coast near present-day Veracruz. He was searching for wealth and had heard rumors of a golden city somewhere in the interior. What Cortés did not know was that the land beyond the rugged mountainous horizon was home to one of the world's great civilizations and perhaps 20 million people. Despite the staggering odds against success, Cortés and his small band of countrymen conquered the fierce and powerful Aztecs. By late summer 1522, Tenochtitlán had fallen, and the vast Aztec Empire was in ruins. A new Spanish-built city, Ciudad de Mexico (Mexico City), rose from the ruins of the former Aztec capital. From the city, Spaniards ruled Nueva España (New Spain, as Mexico was then known), a function Mexico City holds today as Mexico's capital.

Once established on the mainland of Mexico, the Spaniards turned their attention southward—to the vast and powerful Inca Empire. By the late 1520s, the Incan realm was sharply divided and weakened by a bitter civil war that had left the empire in tatters. In addition, an outbreak of smallpox had begun to take a deadly toll on the Incas' population. To add to their troubles, Spanish forces under the command of Francisco Pizarro had arrived on the coast of Peru. With only three ships,

180 men, and 27 horses, they were laying plans to attack one of the world's great empires, with a population of perhaps 6 million people and defended by an army of 30,000 soldiers! When Pizarro finally attacked, victory came brutally and swiftly. His conquest ranks as one of history's greatest military achievements. By 1535, the Spaniards had gained a foothold in Peru, where they founded the city of Lima. This city, located at the foot of the Andes, became the base from which Spaniards would spread much of their growing South American empire.

Moving swiftly northward, the Spaniards settled in Guayaquil, Ecuador, in 1535, and Bogotá, Colombia, by 1538. Sweeping southward, Santiago was founded in Chile's fertile Central Valley in 1541 and La Paz was settled by 1548 in Bolivia's cold and rugged highlands. East of the Andes, the Spanish also established roots in Argentina and Paraguay during the mid-1530s. By 1540, Spain laid claim to most of the Caribbean, Mexico, and Central America, and much of the South American continent. In so doing, they imposed the Spanish language, Catholic faith, a new race of people, and numerous Iberian institutions upon an area nearly 25 times larger than their homeland.

PORTUGAL ENTERS THE COMPETITION

By the mid-1500s, Portugal also had established a foothold in Latin America. Their interests, however, were much different from those of Spain. Spaniards lusted for precious metals, whereas the Portuguese sought land on which to grow sugarcane. Although Brazil later became a major producer of gold, its presence there was unknown during the sixteenth century. In 1541, a small group of Spaniards under the leadership of Francisco de Orellana was sent by Pizarro from Peru down the eastern slope of the Andes in search of gold. No gold was found, but Orellana's party—unable to work their way back up the nearly impassable eastern Andean slopes—did discover the mighty Amazon River and traveled from its headwaters to its mouth. No gold was discovered; hence, Spain showed no interest in what is today Brazil.

In the 1530s, the Spanish founded the city of Lima, Peru, which they used as a staging point to conquer much of South America. Pictured here is the Peruvian Palace of Government, which was built in 1926 and stands on the original site of Governor Francisco Pizarro's house.

Between 1549 and 1561, Portugal established settlements along Brazil's fertile coastal plain, from Recife to Salvador. Fertile alluvial soils, warm tropical temperatures, and ample moisture provided ideal conditions for the growing of sugarcane. Broad expanses of flat land and easy access to oceanic shipping lanes also contributed to the development of huge sugar plantations. Portugal's claim to coastal Brazil was enforced by the earlier Treaty of Tordesillas. Within a decade of Columbus's landfall, Pope Alexander VI of Rome divided the world equally between the Spanish and Portuguese. Although the "line of demarcation" changed through time, it ultimately coincided with

50 degrees west longitude. This north-south line passed through the mouth of the Amazon River, thus giving Portugal legitimate claim to eastern Brazil.

OTHER COLONIAL EFFORTS

During the seventeenth century, other European colonial powers—particularly the British, French, and Dutch—became involved in the competition for lands in the region. Initially, they came as pirates, seeking to plunder Spanish vessels carrying their precious cargo of gold and other riches. Later, they, too, wanted to grow cane and produce sugar. Sugar was in great demand and brought tremendous wealth to its producers. In fact, at one time, the small eastern Caribbean island of Barbados was worth more to the British than all of their holdings combined on the North American continent! Piracy, a problem in earlier centuries, subsided during the latter part of the eighteenth century, as sugar growing expanded. In South America, the British, Dutch, and French established colonies on the northeastern tropical coast—today's Guyana, Suriname, and French Guiana. In Central America, the British established a foothold in what is now Belize. All three countries gained control of various lands in the Caribbean.

SOCIOECONOMIC ASPECTS OF EARLY SETTLEMENT

The Spanish were unaccustomed to hard manual labor; they were not miners and had little interest in farming. To fill the labor void, they turned to the native Amerindian population. Over time, the Spaniards devised a number of systems to ensure an adequate labor force, always at the expense of native peoples. The early dependence on mining and forced labor created a very unhealthy socioeconomic condition, one under which Latin America still suffers. Spanish and Indian populations were brought together, but in a nonharmonious "master and laborer" relationship. Wealth was concentrated in the hands of the very few Spaniards who profited immensely from mining activities. This contributed to a huge gap in wealth and power,

The small 166-square-mile (430-square-kilometer) island of Barbados was and continues to be ideally suited for the growing of sugarcane. At one time, the sugar wealth of Barbados was worth more to the British than the value of all their land holdings in North America. Pictured here is a sugar-processing plant on Barbados.

with the vast majority of people being extremely poor and powerless. The heavy dependence on mineral wealth contributed to economic instability, as tremendous wealth was often followed by grinding poverty, and mines were exhausted and closed. In addition, mining took a terrible toll on the environment. The need for huge amounts of timber resulted in widespread deforestation. Overgrazing of cattle caused massive erosion around most mining communities (livestock was raised for food and also tallow for candles and leather for a variety of purposes). Finally, previously productive Amerindian farmlands ceased producing, as an increasing number of native peoples were taken from their homes to work the mines.

Ultimately, the practice of forced labor contributed to the *hacienda* system that flourished throughout much of Spanish America. In this system, nearly all of the good land was held by a very small number of wealthy Spaniards. Indian laborers made very low wages and normally were deeply in debt (a system very similar to sharecropping in the southern United States after the Civil War). There were many problems with the hacienda system. It hindered the development of a socioeconomic middle class, a condition under which much of Latin America still suffers. Most Spaniards had no experience in, or taste for, farming. Land was a status symbol; that is, it was a source of status rather than of productivity and wealth. Under this system, the vast majority of people were unable to own farmland. This arrangement continued until well into the twentieth century, when in some countries land-reform programs began to redistribute holdings to the poor.

In Brazil, the Portuguese found very few native peoples to work the plantations. They, themselves, were unable (or unwilling) to work the sugar plantations under sweltering tropical conditions. Rather, they needed to find another source of labor. As early as the mid-fifteenth century, Portugal had become involved in the lucrative African slave trade. Beginning in the mid-1600s and lasting for nearly two centuries, a steady flow of African slaves arrived in Brazil to provide labor for the plantations. Today, about 45 percent of all Brazilians can trace their ancestry to African origins.

THE STAGE IS SET

By the end of the eighteenth century, all of Latin America was under the control of European conquerors and colonists. A highly stratified socioeconomic system was solidly in place. Wealth was in the hands of only a few individuals. Most people lived in extreme poverty and were relatively powerless. Few owned land, and the rich hacienda owners used their holdings to gain status rather than wealth from agricultural production. Native peoples had suffered greatly. In many places, their populations had been decimated by warfare and European-introduced diseases against which they had no resistance. Smallpox, influenza, and many other Old World illnesses had taken a dreadful toll. Elsewhere, native peoples had been forced into labor under the most inhumane conditions. Their traditional cultures had been largely destroyed in some areas and were under siege from European-introduced influences in others. In tropical portions of Brazil and throughout much of the Caribbean region, a plantation economy had evolved that depended primarily on African slave labor.

STEPS TOWARD INDEPENDENCE

By the early nineteenth century, many Latin Americans were growing restless. They were becoming increasingly hostile toward what they considered to be heavy-handed control and economic exploitation by the European colonial powers. Three interrelated factors contributed to what ultimately resulted in the wars for independence during the early 1800s: a shift in the balance of power, growing displeasure with Iberian economic policies, and a growing desire for independence.

First was the rising conflict between *Criollos* (Creoles, or people of pure Spanish ancestry born in Latin America) and the *Peninsulares* (those born in Spain). Many Criollos were hacienda or plantation owners whose wealth and position gave them considerable influence. They became unceasingly resentful of and impatient with the Iberian-born Peninsulares, who continued to hold much of the political power. Economics also played an important role. Landowners, merchants, and others in Latin America were becoming increasingly self-sufficient and independent. Spain and Portugal, on the other hand, continued to drain their colonies financially. Latin Americans were particularly unhappy with what they considered to be unfair taxation. Most of the money benefited Iberians, rather than filling local needs. Little attention was given to building schools, hospitals, transportation routes, and other needed public structures. The third factor contributing to a struggle for independence was the rising desire of colonists to be free of European control.

The first two decades of the nineteenth century were a time of great turbulence. Wars for independence raged throughout the region. By 1824, however, all Spanish-held colonies in Latin America had gained their independence. Brazil became independent from Portugal in 1822. In the process, many heroes emerged, none greater, perhaps, than Simón Bolívar, *El Liberator* (The Liberator). Bolívar was a Venezuelan who ultimately became the most powerful leader in the Latin American struggle for independence. Today, people not only in Venezuela, but also Ecuador, Peru, and Bolivia (named in his honor) continue to honor Bolívar for his having helped them gain independence.

Independence came much later to most other European-held colonies. Haiti is a noteworthy exception. There, François-Dominique Toussaint L'Ouverture led a slave revolt that resulted in the colony gaining its independence from France in 1804. In so doing, it became the world's first independent black republic. Most British, Dutch, and other French colonies did not gain their independence until the latter half of the twentieth century. On the South American mainland, Dutch Guiana became the independent country of Suriname in 1975. It was followed by neighboring British Guiana, which became the independent country of Guyana in 1966. Most other British holdings also gained their independence in 1966, although British Honduras (now Belize) did not break away until 1981. The Dutch West Indies became semiautonomous members of the Kingdom of the Netherlands in the 1980s. Former French colonies such as French Guiana, Martinique, and Guadeloupe are now overseas departments of France (a status comparable to being a state within the United States). U.S. interests in the Caribbean include Puerto Rico, which holds commonwealth status, and the unincorporated territory of the Virgin Islands.

LEGACY OF THE COLONIAL ERA

During the colonial era, the foundation was laid for many of the social, economic, and political problems with which most Latin American countries continue to struggle today. Much of the region remains sharply divided along racial, ethnic, and socioeconomic lines. Economically, prosperity remains an elusive dream for many people and most countries, and most governments continue to be corrupt, inept, and largely ineffective. The roots of these problems can be traced to the legacy of sixteenth-century Iberian cultural baggage imposed during the colonial era.

CHAPTER 5

Population and Settlement

Knowing the characteristics of a region's population is perhaps the single most important key to understanding its geographic conditions. It is important to know the number of people living in a given area. Of even greater importance is the distribution and density of population within a region. Geographers also keep a sharp eye on population changes. They seek answers to such questions as, "Why is the population growing in some areas and declining in others?" and, "What is the impact of population change on the affected regions?" It is also extremely important to know the impact population has on a region's economy, government, and environment and how, in turn, these elements may affect the population.

Population can be studied in many ways, but it is most commonly studied demographically and spatially. Demography is the statistical study of the human population. Demographers gather and use such data as the number of people, birth- and death rates, rates of change, life expectancy, migration, and many other aspects of the population. Geographers, on the other hand, emphasize the spatial aspects of demographic conditions. They seek to understand where certain demographic conditions are occurring, why they are happening in certain locations, and the importance of such conditions. Of particular interest to population geographers is human settlement, or the spatial distribution of people. In the United States and many other developed countries, population information is obtained through regularly scheduled censuses. In much of the less developed world, however, the cost of gathering such information is prohibitive. Therefore, statistical population data are often little more than educated guesses.

POPULATION

Latin America is home to approximately 560 million people, or about 8.5 percent of the world's total population. These people inhabit a land area of nearly 8 million square miles (20.7 million square kilometers), giving the region a population density of about 70 people per square mile (27 people per square kilometer). In contrast to the world population density of approximately 125 people per square mile (41 per square kilometer), the region appears to be relatively uncrowded. With regard to their populations, two Latin American countries, Brazil (187 million) and Mexico (107 million), rank number 5 and 11, respectively, among the world's nations. Three of the world's eight largest cities also are in the region—Mexico City (19 million, number 2), São Paulo, Brazil (18.4 million, number 5), and Buenos Aires, Argentina (13.4 million, number 8).

One must be very cautious when interpreting total population data and population density figures. Such information can

From high atop Mount Corcovado, the view of Rio de Janeiro is breathtaking. Brazil's second-largest city is built on a narrow coastal plain, which is backed by a nearly vertical mountain barrier that rises close to 2,000 feet (610 meters).

be very misleading. Rarely does either figure present a clear picture of living conditions or the level of human well-being. Barbados, with a population density of about 1,550 people per square mile (590 per square kilometer), is one of the world's most crowded countries. Yet the tiny Caribbean island enjoys the highest per-capita gross national product (GNP) in all of Latin America. Bolivia, on the other hand, has the lowest population density of any Latin American country, yet it is the region's second-poorest nation.

During the mid-twentieth century, Latin America labored under the world's fastest growing population. In some countries, it was exploding at an annual rate exceeding 3 percent.

Population growth was far outpacing economic gain, contributing to widespread poverty. Today, the rate of natural population increase (RNI) is roughly half that of 50 years ago, a manageable 1.6 percent per year. The RNI is highest in Mexico, Central America, and Bolivia, where it soars well above 2 percent per year. Throughout much of the Caribbean and in Argentina, Chile, and Uruguay, the RNI has fallen below the world average of 1.2 percent yearly.

During recent decades, life expectancy has increased dramatically throughout much of Latin America. Today, it stands at 72 years—5 years longer than the world average. Females live an average of 75 years and males 69. Unfortunately, such averages also can be misleading. Life expectancy drops to 63 years in Guyana and Bolivia, and a shocking 51 years in Haiti. At the other extreme, Costa Ricans can expect to live 79 years. As a general rule, life expectancy relates directly to such indices of well-being as levels of education, quality of hygiene and medical care, and per-capita income.

Age distribution is also a very significant demographic figure. It tells us what percentage of the population is under 15 and over 65. A young population has not yet reached the age of reproduction. This age cohort (group) needs schooling, and as its members age and begin families of their own, the group will need jobs and homes. An elderly population, on the other hand, has retired from the workforce and will need increased medical attention, some means of economic support during its retirement years, and other types of care. Generally speaking, about 29 percent of Latin America's population is under 15 years of age, a number comparable to the world average of 30 percent. Only 6 percent of the population is older than 65, a figure very close to the world average of 7 percent. Again, education, income, and medical care play major roles in determining age distributions. In poor countries such as Haiti and Guatemala, 44 percent of the population is under 15 years of age, but only 4 percent of the people are older than 65. At the other extreme, in well-off Barbados, 22 percent of the people are under 15 and 12 percent are 65 or older.

CHARACTERISTICS OF SETTLEMENT

Settlement refers to where people live, or how the human population is spread out across the land. Many factors influence population distribution. Conditions of the physical environment can influence where people prefer to live or those places that they choose to avoid. The influence of terrain, climate and ecosystems, water features, and soils is quite evident in Latin America's settlement patterns. Numerous cultural factors also must be considered. For example, people tend to settle in places that offer at least some hope of achieving a better quality of life and to avoid those places where living is difficult.

Population distribution in Latin America follows three primary patterns. First, people are very unevenly distributed; the region has several huge clusters of population and also vast areas that support very few people. Second, the region is highly urbanized, with 75 percent of the population living in metropolitan areas. Finally, migration has changed the population distribution and density of many areas.

As can be seen on the "World at Night" image in the front of the book, the most obvious feature of Latin American settlement is its uneven distribution. Population density drops below two people per square mile (one person per square kilometer) throughout nearly half the region. Sparsely populated areas include southern Argentina and Chile, much of the Amazon and Orinoco drainage basins, portions of the Andean Highlands, Guiana, and much of the Brazilian highlands, and portions of arid northern Mexico. In these remote areas, adequate transportation and communication linkages, electricity, and other essential services are scarce to nonexistent. Such areas rarely attract settlers and, because of their isolation and lack of people, are said to be "outside the realm of effective national control." They contribute little to their nation's economy and are difficult to control.

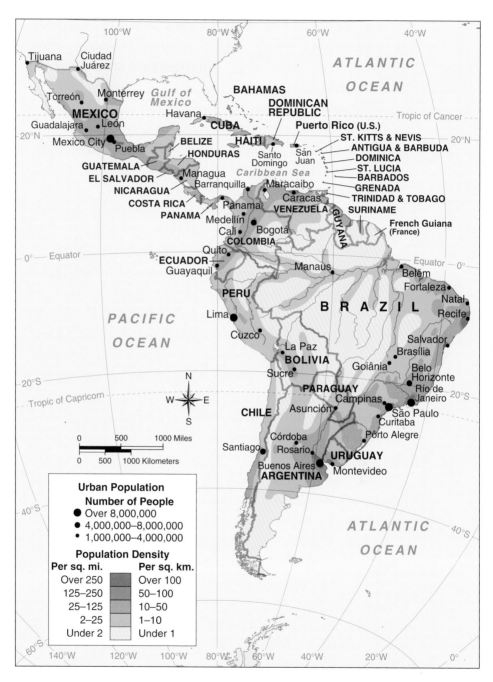

The population of Latin America is unevenly distributed; the coastal regions are densely populated, while the interior regions are largely uninhabited.

Because they are remote, these areas often attract guerrilla or other terrorist groups that are against established governments. Others take advantage of isolation to conduct illegal activities such as the drug trade, poaching, or logging. Disruptive activities such as these are quite widespread throughout much of Latin America. Only three Latin American countries (excluding some small Caribbean islands) have most of their territory effectively settled and easily accessible; these include Uruguay, Costa Rica, and El Salvador. In all other countries, significant areas remain relatively isolated, thinly populated, and poorly developed.

Latin America also has areas with huge clusters of people. In central Mexico, southeastern Brazil, and east-central Argentina, population densities soar to 250 people per square mile (100 per square kilometer) or more. In South America, population tends to be confined to the continent's edges. Nearly 90 percent of the continent's people live within 100 miles (160 kilometers) of the coast. In much of Middle America, on the other hand, the pattern is quite the opposite. There (other than in the Caribbean), people tend to live in the interior, where elevations are higher and the climate somewhat cooler than along steamy tropical coasts.

Although many areas of Latin America support huge population clusters, three in particular stand out. The largest, southeastern Brazil, is home to nearly 85 million people. This booming economic hub is anchored by the inland city of São Paulo, a huge center of industry, agriculture, trade and commerce, and services, with nearly 17 million people in its metropolitan area. Another of the world's great urban centers, Rio de Janeiro occupies a beautiful setting sandwiched between mountains and coast. The city of about 11 million inhabitants is Brazil's center of culture and tourism, as well as its former capital. Other centers include coastal Santos, the port for São Paulo, and Belo Horizonte, a regional center for mining, industry, and agriculture located on the cooler Brazilian Highlands.

To the south, the region's third-largest population cluster, with some 30 million people, surrounds the Rio de la Plata estuary in east-central Argentina and southern Uruguay. Here, the fertile soils and favorable climate of the Argentine Pampas and the rich grazing lands of Uruguay support one of the world's most productive agricultural regions. Metropolitan Buenos Aires (population 11 million) is one of Latin America's major centers of manufacturing and trade. Coastal Montevideo, Uruguay's quiet capital, is home to 1.5 million people. The third huge population cluster is in central Mexico. Here, more than 40 million people live in the crowded area that includes the world's second-largest urban center, Mexico City (estimated population 19 million). Other major cities include Guadalajara and Puebla. Manufacturing, commerce, tourism, and agriculture have long attracted people from Mexico's countryside into the country's bustling heartland.

A HIGHLY URBANIZED POPULATION

Latin America is somewhat unique among the world's less developed regions. Whereas nearly two-thirds of all people in Africa and Asia live in rural areas, fully three-fourths of all Latin Americans live in towns or cities. Worldwide, large urban areas tend to be economically developed—they grow because people can prosper. Throughout much of Latin America, however, economic development and essential services lag far behind explosive population growth. The cities simply lack the industrial, commercial, and service bases to provide jobs or fulfill the other needs of rapidly growing populations. As a result, many urban people live in poverty (as many as 50 percent, in some cities). Landscapes of poverty are very visible in the huge areas of slum settlements (*favelas* in Brazil; *barrios* or *pueblos jóvenes* in Spanish-speaking countries) that surround nearly all large cities within the region. Despite the hardships that many residents endure, urban populations swell as people continue to flee the countryside, clinging to dreams of creating a better life in the cities.

During recent decades, most Latin American cities have experienced explosive population growth, which has outpaced their economic development. As a result, most cities are surrounded by low-income settlements, or slums. In some cities, up to half the population lives without adequate sanitation, clean water, electricity, or other amenities.

Geographers use the term *primate city* in reference to one urban center that is much larger and more important than all others within a country. Such cities tower above all others not only demographically; they also must be a country's political, economic, social, and cultural core. With but few exceptions, most Latin American countries have such a city. Mexico City, Caracas, Bogotá, Lima, Santiago, Buenos Aires, and Asunción far surpass all other cities within their respective countries in terms of their importance. Within Latin America, there are some noteworthy exceptions: Belize (Belize City is the population, economic, and cultural center, but inland Belmopan is the capital); Brazil (capital, Brasilia; population and economic center, São Paulo; cultural heart, Rio de Janeiro); and Ecuador (capital and cultural center in the Andean city of Quito, with the coastal port of Guayaquil the largest city).

PEOPLE ON THE MOVE

Two factors come into play when people decide to move—those that "push" and those that "pull." In Latin America, as elsewhere, a desire to improve one's economic well-being is perhaps the single most important factor influencing peoples' push-and-pull migration decisions. Much of rural Latin America is very poorly developed. Living is difficult. Jobs are scarce, and such essentials as electricity, clean water, and waste disposal are unreliable or nonexistent. So, too, are communication and transportation linkages. Social services, such as adequate schools and healthcare facilities, are generally lacking. Such conditions serve as a strong "push" incentive for people throughout much of rural Latin America. Cities, despite the many hardships often faced by first-generation migrants, offer many "pull" attractions to poor rural peasants. They offer a better standard of living and a much more varied and seemingly exciting lifestyle. During the past century, tens of millions of people have chosen to relocate themselves and their families to cities. This massive rural-to-urban migration has resulted in a major shift in the region's settlement patterns.

Within Latin America, there also have been many migrations affecting regional settlement. In Brazil, about 90 percent of the population inhabited the coastal region. Nearly 50 years ago, the government began implementing several strategies designed to encourage population growth in the country's isolated, sparsely populated, and poorly developed interior. In the 1960s, the seat of government was moved from beautiful Rio de Janeiro to Brasilia, a new city built some 900 miles (1,448 kilometers) inland. The carefully planned city that rose from an empty scrubland plain has grown to a thriving metropolis of about 1.5 million people. In 1966, the port of Manaus—then a sleepy city located on the Rio Negro, near its juncture with the Amazon in the country's interior—was made a free port. In the absence of tariffs, trade boomed, as did the city's population, which expanded fivefold, to nearly 1.5 million. During the past half century, Brazil also has built a network of roads that make it much easier to reach large areas of the once isolated Amazon Basin. Hundreds of thousands of settlers, most of whom were from the poor, arid, and densely settled northeast part of Brazil, have followed these routes into the interior. As the population has grown, so has pressure on the environment. The Amazon rain forest, for example, is being cleared at an alarming rate. Some scientists fear that this cutting and burning to clear land for farming may cause many native plants and animals to disappear.

In the central and northern Andean region, from Venezuela southward to Bolivia, many people are migrating from the highlands into the hot, wet, eastern lowlands. Only in Venezuela, however, has substantial population growth and urban development occurred in these tropical lowlands. Grazing, oil fields, and rich deposits of iron ore and bauxite (the ore from which aluminum is made) have helped this once remote area bordering the Orinoco River grow in importance. In Peru, perhaps 2 million people have been pushed from the Andean Highlands by poverty, poor living conditions, and terrorist activities during the late twentieth century. They have been pulled to the country's primary city, Lima, and other coastal centers.

In Middle America, several major migratory patterns have influenced populations. Most Central American countries have experienced internal migrations resulting primarily from economic influences or, as in during the turbulent last half of the twentieth century, widespread civil unrest. Much of the region also has experienced widespread emigration (outward migration) to Mexico, the United States, and Canada. Many people from the Caribbean have migrated to the United States, Canada, or, in the case of former colonies, to England, France, or the Netherlands.

The greatest ongoing migration in all of Latin America—and in the world today—is from Mexico to the United States. Mexican workers have been migrating to the United States for several centuries, but during recent decades, the flow has gone from a trickle to a flood. Figures are staggering. Today, Latinos (people of Latin American descent, two-thirds of whom have come from Mexico) are the largest minority in the United States. They number 40 million, or about 13.5 percent of the total population. Latinos are also the most rapidly growing segment of the U.S. population. It is estimated that one of every 10 native-born Mexicans now lives in the United States. These figures, however, represent documented residents. By some estimates, another 11 million people (not all from Mexico, of course) are in the United States illegally. Undocumented Mexicans now make up 5 to 6 percent of the U.S. labor force. Clearly, the flow of workers between Latin America and the United States has helped both regions.

ROOM TO GROW

Although most Latin American cities are bursting at the seams, fortunately, the region has ample space in which to grow. In fact, one of the region's major problems is that with rural-to-urban migration occurring at such a rapid pace, rural development is lagging. Difficult environmental conditions can and in some places do pose problems. In most places, however, such obstacles can easily be overcome. It is important to remember that people (their culture, including technology, available capital, and needs), not the environment, determine settlement. It is true that the region has many areas of seemingly "harsh" or "difficult" environmental conditions, but elsewhere in the world, similar environments are home to huge numbers of people.

To be livable, a place must have employment opportunities, easy access, and adequate services. As the Brazilians have shown, for example, when incentives are created, people will follow. Much of the Amazon Basin can be developed, although it must be done in an environmentally sustainable way. The Brazilian Highlands offer some potential for further population growth, as does the Patagonian Plateau. Arid lands, too, can bloom if adequate water resources can be found and diverted. This, of course, can be very costly.

Latin America, unlike many other less developed regions, does not suffer from a burden of overpopulation. Its rate of population growth has been substantially reduced during recent decades, and the region has ample room in which to grow. Throughout most of the region, living standards are improving. There is still a great need, however, for increased political responsibility and stability. If achieved, the regional economy will blossom, bringing further prosperity to Latin America's more than one-half billion people.

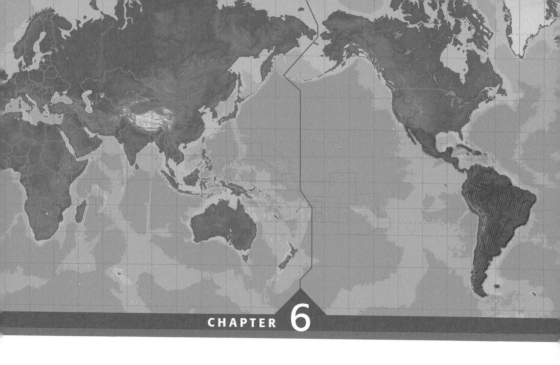

CHAPTER 6

Cultural Geography

Latin America spans a latitudinal distance of about 7,200 miles (11,600 kilometers) from tip to tip, yet one can travel from the U.S.–Mexico border to Cape Horn without leaving a relatively uniform culture. Throughout the journey, the traveler would be "at home" with one language (Spanish), one set of customs (Hispanic), and one religion (Roman Catholicism). He or she would find common values, beliefs, behavioral patterns, and material traits from Tijuana, Mexico, to Ushuaia, Argentina (the world's southernmost city). There is no other area of comparable size in the world in which this could be done. Within this semihomogeneous realm, however, diversity does exist. Portuguese, for example, is the language spoken by the greatest number of people in South America. The Guianas,

Belize, and many Caribbean islands carry the cultural imprint of Northwest European colonial influences. In some regions, Amerindian, African, Asian, or other European traits are dominant. This chapter focuses on Latin America's major cultural similarities and its most striking differences. It also brings attention to the social patterns that have evolved primarily along racial, ethnic, and economic lines.

THE IBERIAN LEGACY

Latin American culture (way of life) grew from roots deeply implanted in the Iberian Peninsula of southwestern Europe. Most of the region carries a strong Spanish imprint, reflecting early Spanish settlement, colonization, and development. In Brazil, of course, the same can be said of Portuguese influence. In both locations, *relocation diffusion* explains existing cultural patterns: Europeans brought their own culture to the New World. Gradually, throughout most of the region, native cultures gave way to new ways of living from far across the Atlantic. Some scholars have referred to this "sixteenth-century cultural baggage" as being the source of many Latin American problems today. Marked differences resulting from historical factors do stand out when one compares and contrasts relative development in Northern (United States and Canada) and Latin America. Some of these differences will be highlighted in their appropriate context within this and following chapters.

LANGUAGE

Language is the single most important trait that binds a population together culturally. Through a common language, a population shares thoughts, ideas, values, beliefs, and knowledge with one another. At the time of conquest, what is now Latin America was home to hundreds of native tongues. Many of these languages ultimately died out, often with their speakers. In some locations, native languages are still dominant. It is estimated that some 40 million people, primarily in the central

Andean area and Central America, speak only a native tongue. Many Amerindian words have been adopted into European languages. This is particularly evident with many of the region's *toponyms* (place names).

Throughout most of the region, Spanish is the primary language. Portuguese is the official language of Brazil. English is spoken in Belize, Guyana, Jamaica, Trinidad and Tobago, and a number of the Lesser Antilles. French is the official language of Haiti, as well as several Overseas Departments of France (French Guiana, Guadeloupe, and Martinique). Dutch is spoken in Suriname and Aruba. In many countries, a number of minority languages still prevail. In Suriname, for example, Sranan Tongo, English, Javanese, and Hindustani join Dutch as the spoken languages. In addition, here and in many other multilingual countries, *pidgin* languages have evolved. A pidgin tongue is a very simple language built from words taken from several languages spoken by people who for various reasons (usually trade) must communicate with one another. A *lingua franca*, on the other hand, is one language that becomes the dominant means of communicating between peoples of diverse tongues. Increasingly, throughout Latin America as elsewhere in the world, English serves this function. Its use is evident in media (music, films, and magazines), computer use, the travel and entertainment industry, trade and commerce, science, and many other activities.

RELIGION

For many cultures, religion and language go hand in hand as influences binding people together. Certainly, this has been true throughout much of Latin America's postconquest history. Most Latin Americans (more than 90 percent of the population) claim membership in the Roman Catholic Church. This figure can be very misleading, however. Today, only 10 to 20 percent of Church members attend services regularly. It is often said, and with some truth, that a "good Catholic" in Latin America

Throughout Latin America, the Catholic faith has left a lasting imprint on the cultural landscape. Churches and cathedrals dominate the skyline of many communities, such as this one in Quito, Ecuador. The most significant structures are usually located adjacent to the plaza in the city center.

attends church three times—his or her baptism, marriage, and funeral.

It is extremely important for Northern American Catholics to realize that the Church in Latin America is vastly different from their own. In many places, Catholicism has been blended with spiritualism and rituals from indigenous or African faiths. In Middle America, animals may be sacrificed on church steps as a part of indigenous rituals. In La Paz, Bolivia, the author has seen kiosks near the cathedral selling dried llama fetuses for use in the rituals of "Popular Catholicism." A huge church in Quito, Ecuador, is segregated (Spanish and Indian), with neon lights decorating the pulpit of the native place of worship.

Popular Catholicism is a blend of Catholic and traditional native doctrine. It varies from place to place and follows no strict doctrine; rather, it depends on local practices. As long as practitioners stick to certain fundamental tenets (rules) of the Church, priests generally allow such practices to continue.

During the European conquest, the role of the Church was much different than it is today. The Church owned much of the better land, was a major slaveholder, and was a primary influence in both government and business. The Inquisition—an institution that practiced brutal torture of "heretics"—was transferred from Iberia to Latin America. Whereas the Inquisition's most visible intent was to keep the region free of non-Catholics, some historians suggest another underlying reason. At the time, much of the potential economic competition was coming from the British and Dutch, who happened to be Protestant. Religion may have been used as the justification for keeping them at bay.

Today, the Church is playing a much more positive role. Rather than supporting the rich and powerful, many priests now speak for the poor and powerless. Unfortunately, those who do so, a practice that has come to be known as "liberation theology," have often been criticized even by the Vatican. Many of the better schools, universities, and hospitals are Church sponsored. Long ago, Latin American law separated church and state, so the current role of the Church is more "religious" than it is political or economic.

Non-Catholic religions also are practiced in Latin America. Hinduism, Islam, and Judaism all claim relatively small numbers of followers. Protestantism is the dominant non-Catholic religion observed in the region today. About 14 percent of all church members in Latin America claim a Protestant denomination as their faith. According to geographer David Clawson, Protestantism in the region is marked by seven characteristics. First, it is gaining ground primarily among the poor rural peasants and urban lower classes. Second, it is dominated by fundamentalism, or very charismatic beliefs and practices. A third feature is an emphasis on unpaid church service, in which church members, rather than clergy members, are responsible for church activities. A fourth characteristic of Protestantism in the region is its small organizational structure. Most congregations have fewer than several hundred members, and most are much smaller. A fifth feature of Latin American Protestantism is that it is primarily indigenous and largely self-governing. That is, local rather than foreign ministers, missionaries, and administers control their own programs. The sixth characteristic is that Protestantism in Latin America is highly fragmented, individualistic, and covetous of its "turf." Strong rivalries and even conflicts often mark relationships between different faiths and their members. Finally, Protestantism is growing rapidly in numbers and strength.

FOOD

What people eat, how it is prepared and by whom, and dining customs are deeply ingrained in each of the world's cultures. A Northern American traveling to Latin America and expecting to find "Mexican food" will be sadly disappointed, even in Mexico! Much of what we in the United States believe to be Mexican food is really Mexican peasant (poor rural farmers) food, and peasants do not eat in restaurants. The diet composed primarily of maize (corn), beans, and meat, consumed with the aid of corn or flour tortillas, is basic to indigenous people in mainland Middle America. What is served in U.S. restaurants as "Mexican" would hardly be recognized or served in any restaurant south of the border.

What is eaten in Latin America depends greatly on location and socioeconomic class. The poor generally eat "peasant" food containing local ingredients and prepared in traditional ways. When traveling, it is always a wonderful experience to dine on this local fare if it can be found. When working in "the bush" (country) in tropical South America, the author has dined on agouti (an aquatic rodent), monkey, manatee, tapir, varieties of fish, various birds, and several "unknown" items. Each experience has added "spice" to his treasured memories of places and people.

Middle and upper classes dine much as we do in the United States and Canada, although some practices differ. In some Latin American countries, for example, the noonday meal is the largest, followed by a *siesta* (nap). Evening meals may be eaten much later than we are accustomed to, as late as 10:00 or 11:00 P.M. in Argentina. Meat, potatoes, rice, vegetables, and wheat bread are staples. Where available, fish and other forms of seafood are popular. In the tropics, plantains, manioc, and other tropical crops are added to the ingredients.

Surprisingly to an outsider, regional diets do vary greatly, and each region has its own specialty or national dish. In Mexico, a variety of wonderful dishes are made with a *mole* (bitter chocolate) base. Argentines, on the other hand, consume more meat per capita than perhaps any other people on Earth. There, barbecue (cooked over a flame) assumes near-sacred proportions. In Peru and Chile, *ceviche* (raw fish, "cooked" in lemon or lime juice) is an extremely popular dish along the coast. In the central Andean Highlands, potatoes of seemingly all colors, shapes, and preparations (including dried) are the basic staple. Here, you may find potatoes accompanying roast cavy (guinea pig). In Brazil, *feijoada* (a black bean stew) is a national dish, as is pepperpot (stew) in Jamaica and several other Caribbean islands. (Space does not allow, but the author urges readers to enter key terms above in a computer search engine and learn more about the dishes and their ingredients. You might even enjoy trying some of them!)

The beverage of choice varies greatly from place to place in Latin America. Throughout most of the region, coffee is king, although in former British colonies, tea is the hot drink of choice. A preferred beverage unique to the region is *yerba mate*, an ancient herbal tea the Europeans adopted from the Amerindians. It is usually drunk from a decorated gourd through a *bombilla*, a silver straw with a sieve at the submerged

Many Latin American countries depend upon coffee as a chief agricultural export. The leading grower is Brazil, which accounts for about 25 percent of the world's total production. Here, coffee beans are being dried in the sun.

end. The drink, initially associated with the gauchos (cowboys), is now popular in southern Brazil, Uruguay, Paraguay, and much of Argentina.

Alcoholic beverages are popular throughout the region. The Roman Catholic Church does not prohibit their consumption. In fact, it was early missionaries who brought winemaking to the region (for use in church services). Today, wine is produced in Argentina, Mexico, and several other countries. The finest wines, however, come from the Mediterranean climate of central Chile. Several of the country's wineries have earned an international reputation for the quality of their products. Many countries have a "national (alcoholic) beverage" made from sugarcane, often consumed straight, or with a squeeze of lime.

Rum, of course, is very popular in sugar-growing areas of the Caribbean. Mexico is famous for its *tequila*, a fermented and distilled beverage made from the agave and maguey plants. Beer is a popular beverage throughout Latin America. Youngsters enjoy a variety of soft drinks and fruit beverages.

WHO IS A "LATIN AMERICAN"?

The obvious answer to the question, "Who is a 'Latin American'?" is, "Anyone who lives in Latin America." Here, however, the reference is to physical appearance, and in this regard, the region provides an array of different human sizes, shapes, and colors. The original inhabitants, Amerindians, were joined through time by Mediterranean Europeans, Africans, Asians, and in some locations northwestern Europeans. The physical appearance of Latin Americans, like that of people from other regions of the world, cannot be stereotyped. They differ greatly from place to place and even within most locations.

Many Amerindians are very short in stature, with an average height of less than 5 feet (1.5 meters). Others are quite tall. Some, such as many highland Indians, are thickset. Others are slender. Some are quite dark in complexion, whereas others are quite light in skin color. Some have the epicanthic fold ("slant" eyes) characteristic of Mongoloid peoples. Others do not. In fact, the great differences in Amerindians' physical appearance suggest different Old World origins and perhaps times of arrival in the Americas. Most people of Spanish or Portuguese origin (Mediterranean Caucasoid) tend to have a slightly darker complexion, and hair and eye color, than most North Europeans. Negroid peoples, who were brought from Africa as slaves, and Mongoloid peoples (Asians) who also came as laborers, resemble people from their source areas. In Latin America, however, it is futile to think in terms of racial "purity." Throughout most of the region, racial intermingling has occurred to such a degree that nearly everyone is of mixed ancestry. In Mexico, Central America, and much of Andean America, the majority of the population is *mestizo* (mixed European and Amerindian ancestry). In Brazil, the Caribbean, and other areas with a large black population, many people are *mulatto* (mixed black and white ancestry). People from Asia were brought to Peru as laborers to work the *guano* (dried bird droppings used as fertilizer) deposits. Today, the Peruvian capital, Lima, boasts 2,000 Chinese restaurants and a thriving Chinatown! People of Asian descent are scattered in small numbers throughout much of Latin America, where many have become successful businesspersons.

In looking once again at the question, "Who is a Latin American?" the diversity can be illustrated by considering data from selected countries. In Argentina, Chile, and Uruguay, more than 90 percent of the population is white. In Jamaica, Barbados, and several other Caribbean islands, 90 percent or more of the people are black. In Honduras, Guatemala, and Bolivia, about 90 percent of the population is Amerindian or mestizo. Between these extremes, most countries have a very diverse population, as is illustrated by Mexico, with 60 percent mestizo, 30 percent Amerindian, 9 percent white, and 1 percent other (primarily Asian).

SOCIAL STRATIFICATION

In Latin America, as is true in nearly all areas of the world, people are separated socially. Many factors can lead such separation into "classes." In some places, race is a factor, in others wealth and position are of greatest importance. Culture and ethnicity determine social class in some countries, whereas family lineage can be important elsewhere. In most societies, combinations of factors determine one's place on the social "ladder." Other factors also are involved; the status of women, age, or vocation (such as that of a priest) weigh heavily in determining social strata.

Because of the widespread racial mixing, prejudice and discrimination (although present) seem to play a less important role in Latin America than they do in many regions of the world. In most of Latin America, a person—regardless of race or ethnicity—can advance himself or herself by "conforming to the rules" of the dominant society. This usually involves education, acquiring a skill, and becoming successful in some occupation. In Mexico, for example, there is a saying that an "Indian becomes a Spaniard when he takes off his sarape, sandals, and sombrero and replaces them with a suit and dress shoes." Until recently, much of Latin American society has been male dominated. During recent decades, however, the role of women has changed greatly. Today, many are well educated, hold positions of importance, and are well respected in their communities. This is particularly true in the cities, whereas many rural women continue to hold traditional family roles.

The social backbone of most industrial and postindustrial countries, such as the United States, Canada, and Western Europe, is a thriving middle class. Unfortunately, throughout much of Latin America, the population remains sharply polarized socioeconomically. This is a legacy of the colonial period. For several centuries, vast wealth was amassed by mining barons and sugar plantation owners. Laborers were slaves or earned very low wages. Wealth, land ownership, and power were in the hands of a few—often only 1 or 2 percent of the population. There were several noteworthy exceptions, such as Chile, Uruguay, and Costa Rica, where no gold or silver was found and there was no plantation economy. In these countries, small farmers developed a very egalitarian (social, political, and economic equality) society. Today, however, most of Latin America continues to suffer from inequality. Wealth and power are held by members of a very small upper class, and the great majority of the people remain poor, poorly educated, and powerless. Developing a strong middle class is one of the great social, political, and economic challenges facing most Latin American countries.

CHAPTER 7

Political Geography

"Turbulent" perhaps best describes Latin American politics since independence. As is true of so many other problems that beset the region, this turbulence can also be attributed to practices and patterns established during the colonial era. A small, but very wealthy and powerful group, supported by the Church, controlled the destiny of most countries. Although the political power of the Church has declined, in the absence of a well-developed middle class, many old practices continue to prevail. Today, all countries including Cuba claim to be republics, states in which leaders are elected and must govern in accordance with constitutional law. By Northern American standards, however, many of them are democratic republics in name only. A tradition of democracy flourishes in only a few places, most notably Chile, Costa Rica, Uruguay, and Barbados, and even these countries have experienced political unrest on occasion.

A TRADITION OF TURBULENCE

Most Latin American countries gained their independence during the early decades of the nineteenth century. Since then, the region's political history has resembled a very bumpy roller coaster ride. Since independence, Ecuador's presidents have averaged just over two years in office, and the country has averaged a new constitution every four years. Strife-torn Bolivia has experienced about 200 *coups d'etat* (violent overthrows of a government)—more than one a year. In 1970, the country had three presidents in three days. Even this staggering figure pales in comparison to Argentina, however, which during a two-week period in 2002 had five different presidents!

A POLITICAL "CYCLE OF FRUSTRATION"

A "cycle of frustration" can help us better understand the instability of politics and government in Latin America. The "cycle" shows how numerous factors interact with one another to make governing very difficult in most of the region's countries.

Native Cultural Heritage

At the time of European conquest, the Americas were home to millions of native peoples. The conquest, itself, set the stage for deep conflict between the two groups. Amerindians, themselves, often were in conflict with one another. Spaniards (the Portuguese came in contact with very few native peoples in Brazil) immediately conquered, dominated, and both used and abused native populations. Native lands were taken and settlements destroyed. Centuries later, many native peoples remain poor, uneducated, and relatively powerless. During recent decades, however, they have spoken with increasingly loud voices of protest. People of Amerindian ancestry have been elected president in a number of countries, and Amerindian protests have been responsible for the overthrow of governments in several others. Increasingly, they are a "thorn in the side" of the governments in power. After being "voiceless" for centuries, today native issues and concerns must be heard and acted upon.

European Cultural Heritage and Influence

Reference has previously been made to the "sixteenth-century Iberian 'cultural baggage'" that Spaniards and Portuguese imposed upon the newly settled lands. Until recent decades, Mediterranean Europe suffered from political instability. This tradition of strong leaders governing with an iron fist and without democratic process is what the Iberians brought with them to the Americas. The system that evolved in Latin America very much resembled the old European feudal system. It was one in which a small handful of very wealthy and powerful people governed the poor and powerless masses. This system prevails today in many Latin American lands. The obvious result is growing dissent by the masses toward the existing political system and government in power.

Natural Environment and Resource Base

The region's natural environment poses some problems to development, but it also offers many potentials. Developing such potentials—opening new lands to settlement, building transportation and communication linkages, developing tourism, bringing land into agricultural production, and so forth—requires capital. Most Latin American countries, however, simply lack the financial resources for such development, and foreign business interests are generally reluctant to risk investing in countries with unstable governments.

In some areas, environmental conditions have imposed huge barriers to transportation and economic development. The Andes, for example, divide Venezuela, Colombia, Ecuador, Peru, and Bolivia. Each of these countries has an area that is accessible,

In recent years, natives have voiced their concerns over being treated unfairly by Latin American governments. Pictured here are several Mapuche Indians, who marched more than 400 miles (643 kilometers) to demand land and better living conditions from the Chilean government.

densely settled, and economically developed. But each of them also has a huge area of "frontier" that lies well beyond reach of easy access and control. One major problem facing many Latin American countries is the lack of fossil fuels—coal, petroleum, and natural gas. This means that money spent on fuel imports is not available to invest in domestic development.

Economic Conditions

Most of Latin America falls squarely within the category of nations identified as being "less developed" economically. Per-capita incomes and gross national products rank slightly below the world average. Many countries are still in the process of undergoing the transition from an agricultural economy to one based on industry and services. However, primary industries—mining, farming or livestock grazing, logging, fishing, and other extractive activities—still dominate most regions. Further, many countries have *monoeconomies*. They rely on a single item for the majority of their wealth. When the commodity is a nonrenewable resource—such as petroleum in Venezuela or copper in Chile—the problem is even greater. When reserves are exhausted, the country's economy is left in shambles. It also can happen with agriculture. Most Central American "Banana Republics" sank into economic despair when diseases wiped out the banana industry in the 1930s.

Finally, through time, many of Latin America's precious natural resources have been extracted for the benefit of others. Most of the gold and silver went to Spain, and Brazil's sugar to Portugal. Today, much of the region's mineral and other resource wealth is in the hands of foreign corporations and is exported. It is impossible for a government to provide adequate services for the people if it lacks sufficient financial resources to do so, and in the absences of such services, people become restless and critical of their government and its leaders. They want and need good transportation and communication networks, adequate schools and health-care facilities, and police protection.

Infrastructure

An adequate infrastructure—a network of highways, railroads, power grids, ports, and other systems of movement and delivery—are essential to any country's development. Throughout much of Latin America, these facilities are woefully inadequate. In some areas, physical obstacles—such as rugged mountains or numerous rivers—make construction difficult and extremely costly. Many areas are poorly developed and support a low population density and, therefore, do not warrant the cost of building roads, power lines, or other facilities.

Maps showing highways and railroads in Latin America reveal several very tight clusters that stand in sharp contrast to vast areas with little if any surface access. The greatest density of highways and railroads, as would be expected, are in heavily populated and industrialized southern Brazil and northeastern Argentina. Facilities also are adequate in central Mexico. In the Andes, however, no highway or railroad crosses the range between Colombia and southern Peru—a distance of more than 2,000 miles (3,200 kilometers). The Amazon Basin occupies an area roughly the size of the 48 contiguous U.S. states. There is no railroad, and only two relatively unimproved roads span the vast area, one north–south and another east–west, well to the south of the Amazon River. In the Amazon, travel is either by boat on the many rivers, or by air.

Clearly, if Latin America is to prosper, the infrastructure must be greatly improved. There is little integration of systems; that is, with but few exceptions (such as the Pan American Highway), railroads and highways do not join countries. In fact, each country has a different rail gauge (width between the tracks). This was done deliberately in order to ensure that the military of hostile neighbors could not enter the country by rail. Building an adequate infrastructure is primarily the responsibility of a nation's government. Unfortunately, most Latin American countries are barely able to meet more pressing demands such as education and health care.

Settlement Patterns

Settlement was discussed in detail in Chapter 5. In terms of its political impact, the region's settlement patterns impose several critical problems on its governments. First, the region is home to some of the world's largest cities, and fully 75 percent of the population is urban. Unfortunately, most cities lack the financial resources to keep pace with urban growth. Huge slums ring nearly all the region's cities. Services are poor or lacking. Schools and hospitals are inadequate. Air and water pollution and sanitation rank among the world's worst. Under such conditions, urban unrest is an omnipresent problem for both municipal and federal governments.

A second problem is created by the vast areas within most countries that support few people, experience little development, and have limited access. Such areas obviously contribute very little to a country's economy. Adding to this problem is the widespread rural-to-urban migration. As people leave their rural homes, they further drain the countryside of human resources and economic potential. They also add to the population of cities that are already overcrowded. Governments must work to develop their countries' rural areas, and living conditions in the countryside must be greatly improved in order to make rural living more pleasant.

Population Patterns, Conditions, and Trends

Throughout most of the twentieth century, Latin America's population grew at a rate that outstripped economic growth. Poverty and illiteracy were widespread. The region suffered from severe "overpopulation"—more people than a nation's economy can provide for adequately. Much of the political instability—dictators, military governments, and seemingly constant political pressure and turmoil—experienced during the last century can be attributed to this problem. People simply were increasingly desperate and impatient.

Today, population growth is one of Latin America's "bright spots." The rate of increase has dropped nearly 1.5 percent over

The Organization of American States (OAS) is made up of 35 countries in both North and South America and seeks to defend democracy, protect human rights, and strengthen regional security. Pictured here is César Gaviria, who served as secretary general of the OAS from 1994 to 2004, at the 32nd Regular Session of the OAS General Assembly in Bridgetown, Barbados, in 2002.

the past four decades, to its current rate of 1.5 percent per year. In most countries, the rate of economic growth is now greater than that of the population. This means that per-capita gross national products and per-capita incomes are gaining each year.

POLITICAL REALITIES AND CHALLENGES

Today, most Latin American countries are politically more stable than at any time in their history. Regionally, they are joined together by the Organization of American States (OAS), the world's oldest regional alliance of countries. The OAS seeks to strengthen cooperation and advance the common interests of member nations. High on its agenda are defending democracy, protecting human rights, and strengthening regional security.

It also works to promote free trade among member countries, combat the illegal drug trade, and fight corruption. Globally, all countries hold active membership in the United Nations. From 1982 to 1991, Peruvian diplomat Javier Pérez de Cuéllar held the post of UN Secretary General. All countries also hold memberships in numerous other international agencies. Brazil is a member of 61 international organizations, whereas tiny Antigua and Barbuda, with a population of 69,000, holds membership in 34. Today, Latin America plays an ever-increasing role on the world stage.

Despite the current political stability, the region faces many challenges. Fidel Castro's Cuba remains the only Communist state in the Western Hemisphere. Many observers believe that Haiti simply cannot be governed effectively. In 2005, Venezuelan president Hugo Chavez appeared to be drifting far to the left. There are some fears that he will follow in Castro's footsteps in taking his oil-rich country down a Marxist path. Ecuador, Peru, and Bolivia continue to drift between political stability and chaos. Several things are certain: The region must reduce growing political (and business) corruption, the rampant drug trade that affects many countries must be curtailed, and governments must play a much more active role in improving services and living conditions for Latin Americans.

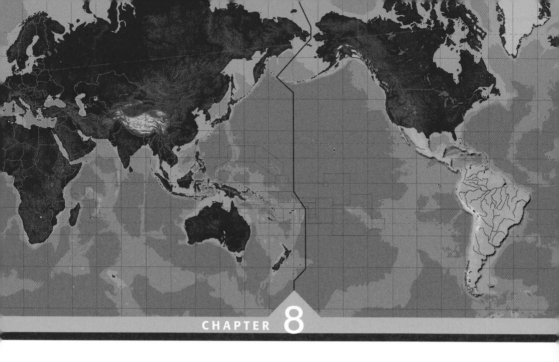

CHAPTER 8

Economic Geography

Economically, most if not all of Latin America falls within the category of the Less Developed Countries (LDCs). During recent decades, however, much of the region has made remarkable progress in terms of economic development. In 2005, the per-capita gross national income purchasing power parity (GNI-PPP) was nearly $7,600. The figure represents the amount of goods and services the same money could buy in the United States.

Prosperity, however, varies greatly from place to place. In South America, Argentineans and Chileans enjoy a GNI-PPP four to five times greater than residents of Bolivia or Ecuador. A considerable gap also exists in Central America. The GNI-PPP in Costa Rica and Mexico is two to three times greater than in much less developed

Honduras and Nicaragua. With the exception of Haiti, which is one of the world's poorest countries, the Caribbean region enjoys the highest incomes. In Barbados, Trinidad and Tobago, Puerto Rico, Guadeloupe, and Martinique, the GNI-PPP is approaching the threshold of developed countries. (Note: Specific figures for each country, updated annually, can be found in The CIA World Factbook: *http://www.cia.gov/cia/publications/-factbook/index.html*

AN ECONOMIC "CYCLE OF FRUSTRATION"

Many factors help explain these marked regional differences in economic well-being. As you learned in the previous chapter, political stability or lack thereof is perhaps the single most important factor helping explain such differences. A "cycle of frustration" was used to explain the many problems that confront Latin American governments. The same approach can be useful in helping to gain a better understanding of the region's economic conditions.

Native Cultural Heritage

The map on page 99 that shows levels of economic development in Latin America reveals some startling differences. With but few exceptions, areas of poverty coincide with the distribution of Amerindian (or African American) populations.

In order to understand this problem, one must turn to cultural differences. Most native cultures are only now beginning to emerge from a *folk economy*. They follow traditional folkways in farming, herding, or other economic pursuits. Exchange is often by barter rather than cash based. Traditional cultures are quite self-sufficient. They do for themselves those things that most of us pay others to do. As measured by their own culture's values, they may be very comfortable and well-off, but none of their work can be measured financially; hence, they appear to the outsider to be poor.

One definition of *education* is "knowledge for survival." Many of the folk have an intimate (one might say "brilliant") understanding of how to hunt, fish, farm, or otherwise provide for their families, but they do not need a formal education to contribute in this way. Contemporary "modern" society, on the other hand, demands literacy—the ability to read, write, and use mathematics. As a result, many traditional societies are ill-prepared to participate in urban-industrial-commercial economic activities.

European Cultural Heritage

As was mentioned in several earlier chapters, the Iberians introduced a feudal system many centuries ago, and in Latin America, old traditions have been difficult to break! Wealth has always been in the hands of a very few, leaving most of the population quite poor. Even today, a strong middle class has emerged in only a few countries. The Spaniards and Portuguese also brought another tradition that seems very strange to most Northern Americans—avoidance of work. Hard work, particularly manual labor, was to be avoided by a *caballero* (gentleman). Although the belief is beginning to disappear, particularly in cities, it imposed a severe handicap on economic development.

Natural Environment and Resource Base

In economic terms, the natural environment does present some problems. Tropical soils tend to be infertile, wet tropics and desert regions both impose certain problems on settlement and development, and mountains and rivers create barriers to the building of integrated transportation networks. The environment also offers much potential. There are huge areas of excellent soil; throughout most of the region the climate is mild and free of such devastating storms as tornadoes and hurricanes; in many areas, spectacular scenery can serve as the basis for tourism. Latin America is no better or worse off than most regions of the world in terms of what the natural environment offers. Cultural geographers realize that there really are no unproductive regions, but there are people who do not take advantage of what they have.

Throughout most of their history, the economies of Latin America have depended on the region's rich and diverse natural resources. Native peoples farmed the land, hunted and fished, and mined precious metals. Spaniards turned to the huge stores of gold and silver for wealth; Portuguese and other colonizing European nations turned to the region's fertile soils. Neither mineral wealth nor soils are evenly distributed throughout Latin America. Some countries are rich in one but poor in the other. A few countries, such as Mexico, Brazil, and Chile, are rich in both. The one thing that most Latin American countries lack is a store of fossil fuels. Mexico and Venezuela are major producers of petroleum, and several other countries have small deposits. There is very little coal.

Infrastructure

Economic development and a good network of transportation and communication facilities go hand in hand, yet much of Latin America lacks a well-integrated system of highways, railroads, and communications. Most areas surrounding large cities are well served, but vast land areas of most countries lack easy access. Such regions generally contribute little to a country's economy.

Settlement Patterns

Several characteristics stand out with regard to the distribution of Latin America's settlement and its importance. First, it is highly urbanized. People flock to the cities in hope of improving their standard of living. Urban growth has far outstripped economic development in many urban centers. As a result, cities fester with encircling slums and unemployment rates that

Most rural Latin Americans continue to live conventionally, relying primarily upon farming to make a living. This Mexican farmer is using a traditional "ard" type of plow drawn by a yoke (team) of oxen.

often exceed 50 percent. Second, as people flee the countryside, it becomes increasingly difficult to develop the economic potential of rural areas (and, of course, with fewer people residing in outlying districts, there is less incentive to spend resources to develop them).

Population

Throughout much of its history, population was growing faster than the economy in Latin America. Poverty was widespread and it seemed as though economic development would never catch up. During recent decades, however, the rate of population growth has dropped sharply and the economy has strengthened. Today, most Latin American countries are experiencing an annual rate of economic growth that exceeds that of their population gain. In Mexico, for example, the population is growing at a rate of about 1.2 percent, whereas the economy is increasing at 4.1 percent (2005). Brazil's population is increasing by about one percent each year, but its economy is gaining at a rate of just more than 5 percent annually. In both countries, the economy is outstripping population gain; hence, each year the people are better off financially. In Haiti, however, the population is growing by 2.3 percent each year, whereas the economy is actually declining by 3.5 percent a year (in 2005). You can see how this contributes to increased poverty among the country's already desperately poor people.

Government

Here, we go full cycle and link government and politics to economics. Again, the two go hand in hand. In those countries that enjoy political stability, the economy generally grows and the people prosper. In lands served by inept, corrupt, and ineffective governments, the economy, and therefore the people, suffer.

ECONOMIC ACTIVITIES

Geographers have identified several types of economic activity. The most common method is based on what people actually do to make a living. Some jobs, such as mining, lumbering, fishing, and farming, are based on extracting something from the natural environment. They require considerable skill and much physical labor but little formal education. Workers in these industries generally have low incomes. Jobs, and therefore workers, are tied to one place. People working in these *primary industries* often have a very limited awareness of the "outside" world.

People engaged in providing professional services represent the opposite extreme. *Service industries* include managers and executives, educators, people in the medical field, attorneys, and other service providers. A formal education and considerable knowledge and skill are needed to be successful in these fields. The jobs usually pay quite well, and people involved in service industries usually enjoy considerable freedom and mobility. Whereas the world of many people in the primary industries stops at their horizon, people engaged in service industries must possess a detailed "mental map" of the region and world. Today, nearly any place in the world can be reached in a day. People and materials move about within an increasingly global community. The world has been brought together as one giant neighborhood by computers and satellite communications. Using the Internet, people can obtain current information from across the globe. These developments have changed the way business is done worldwide.

For economically disadvantaged countries, and people unprepared to compete, meeting the challenges of the new global economy can be a daunting task. Fortunately, literacy rates throughout much of Latin America are quite high, exceeding 90 percent in most countries and approaching 99 percent in some. This gives the region a solid base of human resources from which to develop. The following section provides a brief overview of how Latin Americans make their living as workers in *primary* (resource extraction), *secondary* (manufacturing), and *tertiary* (service and management) industries.

Primary Industries

Primary industries are directly involved with the use of natural resources, such as fishing, mining, logging, and agriculture. In the United States, these industries face critical challenges from environmental groups. In much of Latin America, however,

these extractive industries are seen as a way of improving strug-
gling economies. In fact, from the outset of European settlement, mining and agriculture have been the region's chief
economic activities. In the United States, only about 2 percent
of the population is engaged in primary industries. In Latin
America, the figure is much higher. In some of the less developed and less urban countries, such as Haiti and Guatemala,
nearly two-thirds of the population is engaged in primary economic activities. In the better developed and more urban lands,
such as Argentina, Barbados, and Chile, the figures are
comparable to that of the United States.

Mineral Extraction

Since colonial times, mining has been the economic backbone of
many countries. The mines of Mexico, Bolivia, Peru, and other
lands pumped billions of dollars of wealth into the coffers of
Spanish royalty and later local economies. Today, many countries still rely on mineral resources as their primary source of
wealth. In fact, nearly three-fourths of all Latin American countries depend on mineral extraction for more than 50 percent of
their gross domestic product (GDP). In Venezuela, Mexico, and
Ecuador, petroleum provides the bulk of national income. Chile
depends heavily on the production of copper, and Bolivia on a
host of minerals, the most important being tin. Brazil, Jamaica,
Suriname, and Guyana are major producers of bauxite, the ore
from which aluminum is made. Elsewhere in the region, iron,
tin, lead, and zinc are locally important. Although most deposits
of precious metals have long been exhausted in many of the for-
merly Spanish-held lands, Brazil has become a major producer
of gold during recent decades.

Mineral extraction creates three major problems. First, it
tends to contribute to a boom-and-bust economy. What will
happen to the economy of Venezuela when the petroleum
is gone, Chile when the copper plays out, or Bolivia when
its mines close? Second, in mining, the resulting wealth often

Resources

- ✗ Coal
- ◇ Diamonds
- ⚡ Hydroelectric power
- ⚖ Iron
- ◊ Natural gas
- ⚒ Petroleum
- ▱ Precious metals (gold, silver, copper)
- ❋ Uranium

Land Use

- ▮ Hunting and gathering
- ▯ Subsistence farming
- ▮ Commercial farming
- ▮ Nomadic herding
- ▮ Grazing
- ▮ Commercial fishing
- ▮ Forestry
- ▮ Trade and manufacturing
- ▯ Little or no activity

Since the time of European settlement, the primary industries of Latin America have been mining and agriculture. Today, other key industries include the manufacturing of textiles and additional consumer goods.

benefits only a small number of people. Those in control gain huge profits, but the miners themselves and the public at large, rarely share in the revenue. Finally, in most countries there are few environmental controls, resulting in widespread air and water pollution and spoiling of the land.

Fishing

The Atlantic and Pacific oceans yield an abundance of fish, shellfish, and crustaceans. Archaeological evidence from coastal Peru suggests that as early as 3000 B.C., coastal peoples depended on harvesting the rich marine resources. Native peoples living at the tip of South America also depended on shellfish and other marine life as their primary source of food. In many coastal countries, seafood plays a prominent role in the regional diet. The same can be said for people living along the Amazon River and its many tributaries. An early morning visit to a fish market in Iquitos, Manaus, Belem, or elsewhere along a major stream reveals an incredible variety of freshly caught delicacies. On occasion, Peru has ranked number one among the world's fishing nations. Today, some countries are even "farming" such commercially valuable species as shrimp and salmon.

Logging

Much of Latin America suffered from deforestation for decades, if not centuries. Woodlands were cut for fuel, mining timbers, rail ties, and many other uses. The result was (and continues to be) widespread erosion, local flooding, and land degradation. The problem is particularly acute in Haiti, portions of Central America, and Andean South America. Lumber, pulp, paper, and other industrial products depend on the logging industry. Today, of course, the entire world is keeping a watchful eye on forest clearing in the Brazilian rain forest.

The Amazon Basin is home to one of the world's three great forests. During recent decades, however, this environmental treasure has been under increasing attack. Because much of the forest is softwood, which is of little economic value, most of the timber is simply cut and burned. Land-hungry peasants plant crops on the cleared land, but as you learned in Chapter 2, residual tropical soils become infertile after several years. Consequently, the farmers move on and the cycle of clearing, farming, and abandoning the land continues.

Agriculture

If you ate a banana or other tropical fruit, or enjoyed coffee or orange juice made from frozen concentrate with your breakfast, the odds are that you can thank a Latin American farmer. The same holds true for much of our winter produce, including tomatoes, onions, and asparagus, and many of the flowers we can enjoy during the winter months. Much of the region has a market advantage because it is tropical or south of the equator— residents there are enjoying summer while we shiver through winter. Throughout much of Latin America, agriculture has long been the primary industry, involving the greatest number of people. Farming has been mainly for subsistence; that is, people raise crops for their own use. From the very outset of European settlement, however, some crops—like sugarcane, and later coffee—were grown for export. Brazil was the world's leading producer of cane sugar, and sugarcane was the lifeblood of many Caribbean islands. Later, Brazil became the world's leading producer of coffee. Today, coffee is an important export from a number of Latin American countries, including Colombia, Guatemala, and Jamaica, which is famous for its very high-quality (and expensive—it can run as much as $36 per pound!) Blue Mountain coffee.

During the twentieth century, commercial agriculture became more diversified and important to the economy of many countries. Chile is famous for its excellent wines; Brazil has become a leading producer of soybeans; and Argentina, once the world's leading exporter of agricultural products, continues to be a major producer of grains and other basic crops. The banana industry, after decades of shifting southward to Ecuador because of disease, is once again thriving in much of Central America. Bananas and other tropical crops are an economic mainstay of many Caribbean islands, as well. Northern Mexico has become a major grower of produce destined for U.S. tables.

The Spaniards introduced livestock ranching into Latin America during the early sixteenth century. Today, it is a booming industry throughout much of the region. If you enjoyed a hamburger from a fast-food restaurant for lunch, quite probably the meat came from Latin America.

Secondary Industries

Secondary industries are those that take primary materials and turn them into something useful by processing or manufacturing. Examples include any manufacturing or building industries, food processing industries, and energy production. Smelting ore and making steel, refining petroleum and producing gasoline, and producing textiles and making clothing all fall within this category.

Latin America, despite its extensive urbanization, entered the Industrial Revolution late. In fact, industrialization lags in much of the region even today. Some areas, such as around Mexico City and Monterrey in Mexico, São Paulo in Brazil, and Buenos Aires in Argentina, are heavily industrialized and have been for some time. Puerto Rico, based primarily on American markets, capital, and management, also has prospered from extensive industrial development. During recent decades, several thousand industries have clustered on the Mexican side of the U.S.–Mexico border. These *maquiladora* plants depend largely on an abundant supply of cheap labor and lax environmental laws. Industries (most of which are American owned) deliver parts to the factories in Mexico; these parts are then assembled into finished products. The components are returned to the United States as finished products but built at a considerably lower cost than if they were manufactured domestically. Today, much of the world's second-

Much of Latin America lags in steel production, with only Mexico and Brazil having large, integrated mills. Pictured here is the huge mill in Volta Redonda, Brazil, which was founded in 1941. The site was selected because of its proximity to Rio de Janeiro and São Paulo and because there are nearby power sources and raw materials needed to manufacture steel.

ary economic activity is bypassing Latin America. China, India, and other Asian countries offer comparably low wages and often turn out higher quality products.

Tertiary and Other Related Activities

Today, more Latin Americans are engaged in tertiary, or service-related, activities than ever before. Many people are engaged in wholesale or retail sales. Professional people, such as teachers, professors, attorneys, and anyone involved in any aspect of health care fall within this category. So, too, do entertainers and athletes, police and military, and clergy and politicians.

Tourism is perhaps the Latin American tertiary industry with which Northern Americans are most familiar. Although well developed in some areas, tourism holds tremendous untapped potential throughout much of the region. Tourism thrives in much of the Caribbean and in parts of Mexico. Sadly, tourist visits (and dollars) are subject to huge fluctuations within the region. When tales of murder, drug gangs running rampant, political riots, beatings, extortion, and kidnappings reach the attention of potential tourists, it is not surprising that they select another vacation spot! First and foremost, the region must ensure that visitors will be safe. Much of Latin America offers fantastic natural beauty, marvelous historical treasures, and fascinating cultural practices. But travel costs can be very high, and tourist facilities are often poor to nonexistent. This is one area in which much can be done to improve local economic conditions.

TRADE AND COMMERCE

All countries have something of value that they produce. It may be in the form of natural resources or raw materials. As you have seen, many Latin American nations have mineral wealth, are producers of agricultural commodities, or both. Production may also be in the form of manufactured or processed goods. Mexico's maquiladoras assemble thousands of different items, Chile's vineyards produce wonderful wines, and plants throughout much of the region manufacture articles of clothing. Still other areas provide special services, such as processing manufacturers' coupons or credit card data. Each of the foregoing can be exported. Export revenue helps not only individuals and businesses but countries as well. Their income, in turn, is used to pay for goods and services on which they depend. All countries also need various materials, products, or services that cannot be provided domestically. They must turn to imports. These exchanges form the foundation upon which trade and commerce are built.

Think for a moment about those things that you have, use, or consume. How many can you identify that are from Latin

America? What about Japan, China, South Korea, or elsewhere in Asia? Your answers may have provided you with an essential key to understanding today's global economy. Chances are that you could think of very few things, if any, from Latin America. If you did, they were almost certainly low-cost items, such as agricultural products. Now, what about Asia? Did you list an automobile, motorcycle, or other sport vehicle? How about electronic items such as a television, stereo, or CD player? Did you find cameras, watches, precision tools, or other high-value items? In which region—Latin America or eastern Asia—is labor the best educated, the most skilled, and highest paid? Which region benefits the most from trade? Which region has more capital available to import needed goods from elsewhere? In which region do people have at least the opportunity to improve themselves financially? You now understand why Latin America falls behind many of the world's other developing areas.

Trade within Latin America has always lagged. Only recently have a variety of mutual trade agreements begun to lower trade barriers, such as tariffs. In 1994, the North American Free Trade Agreement (NAFTA) was signed between the United States, Canada, and Mexico. So far, however, trade between Mexico and its northern neighbors has been somewhat limited. More recently, in August 2005, a new free trade agreement (CAFTA) was signed by the U.S. president; it includes the Central American countries and the Dominican Republic. Latin America still has a very long way to go, however, before it becomes a major player on the global economic stage.

ECONOMIC ISSUES

Overall, the Latin American economy is in desperate need of a "jump start." In the section of this chapter focusing on the "cycle of frustration," you learned that the success or failure of an economy is the result of many complex and interconnected factors. First and foremost, the region needs to achieve political stability.

It must attract foreign capital, and its own citizens must feel secure in investing in their own country's development.

The "shadow economy," or regional and international illegal drug trade, is a major problem confronting numerous Latin American countries. It appears to be particularly critical in the central and northern Andean region, Mexico, and Jamaica. Revenues are undocumented and, of course, untaxed. The human toll is immense. Much of the political instability in those countries affected can be attributed to the growing, processing, and trade of illegal drugs. Problems include rampant corruption, terrorist-spawned mayhem, devastating civil conflict, and the cancerous criminal activity that combine to eat away at a country's economic potential.

Unemployment remains a huge problem throughout much of Latin America. For the region as a whole, it hovers around 10 percent, but the figure varies widely from country to country. Of equal concern is *under*employment, people who hold jobs but are unable to make an adequate living. An alarmingly high percentage of the region's population struggles to make ends meet because their income is so low. In Haiti, for example, 80 percent of the population lives below the poverty level. In all but a few countries, fully half to three-fourths of the people fall within this category. Incomes and living standards must be improved.

As Latin America looks to the future, it faces no greater task than to achieve political stability, which, in turn, will lead to economic growth within the region.

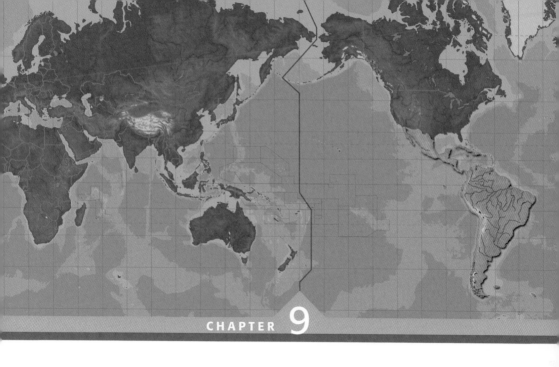

CHAPTER 9

Latin America Looks Ahead

Latin America is a region that possesses many strengths and potential but also a number of glaring weaknesses and obstacles. Looking ahead is a task fraught with uncertainty. The fickle winds of change are extremely difficult to forecast. Geographers have long looked to the past to understand the present and to glimpse the future. Past and current trends can be particularly revealing in this regard.

We know from the past, for example, that natural forces will continue to wreak havoc on large areas of the region. The Caribbean will continue to be devastated by hurricanes, and seismic activity will continue to rattle the mountainous areas bordering the Pacific Ring of Fire. Within this same region, volcanic eruptions, rock avalanches, and earth flows will continue to take a heavy toll on life and property.

Drought will continue to plague some areas, whereas others drown beneath floodwaters. Deforestation will continue to cause hot debate in the Amazon Basin, Central America, and elsewhere.

Latin America's varied natural landscapes and conditions also offer great potential. The relatively recent boom in eco-tourism—visiting and enjoying natural landscapes such as Costa Rica's humid tropical national park system—offers huge potential. Most if not all countries have something within their natural environment that can be further developed as a tourist attraction.

Throughout much of the twentieth century, Latin America sagged under an extremely high rate of natural population increase (for a time, the world's highest). Today, the rate of gain has dropped by nearly half, to a manageable 1.5 percent. In most countries, the economy is growing at a rate considerably greater than the population. During recent years, nearly every country has experienced sustained improvement in the standard of living of its people, as measured by per-capita income. Three of every four Latin Americans live in a city. Urban centers, already bursting at the seams, must develop the economic base and infrastructure of services that will support these populations. Many rural regions of Latin America offer tremendous potential for economic development and additional human settlement. As this occurs, a watchful eye must be kept to ensure that it occurs in a way that is environmentally sustainable.

Latin American culture and society are undergoing considerable change, and this momentum will almost certainly continue into the future. The transition from a subsistence level folk economy to a modern cash economy has been slow, but today it has spread throughout most of the region. With this change, the great majority of Latin Americans have been formally educated, and literacy rates are high. Schools, as well as educational facilities and opportunities, must be improved, but this is gradually occurring as funding becomes available. The greatest challenge confronting Latin American society is the development of a strong middle class. Five centuries after the

Although many Latin American nations have developed strong economies in recent years, there are still areas that tend to lag behind the large urban regions. Pictured here are children from the rural province of Misiones who have marched to Buenos Aires to ask the Argentinean government for food, better health care, and more jobs for their parents.

European conquest, most countries still have a sharply polarized society. Wealth and power are in the hands of a few, and the great majority of people are poor and without a strong voice in determining their own destiny. Throughout most of Latin America, the middle class is growing. For many of the region's more than one-half billion people—including its minority populations—progress is painfully slow.

During the past half century, Latin America has made remarkable progress politically. With the exception of Fidel Castro, no country suffers under a strong-arm dictator. In the mid-1950s, most countries were dictatorships, and by the 1970s, much of the region was in turmoil. Terrorist groups and civil conflicts were widespread. This left economies in shambles and societies sharply divided and in tatters. During recent decades, however, most countries throughout the region have become democracies (at least in name). Most terrorist threats are diminished and with few exceptions, civil strife has subsided. People are beginning to insist on good government and to hold their leaders accountable. This offers considerable hope for an increasingly stable future for most if not all the region's countries.

Although most countries rank among the world's less developed, considerable economic progress has been made within the region as a whole. Only a few lands, such as Haiti and Cuba, continue to show little economic growth. As has been mentioned throughout this book, economic stability and economic growth go hand in hand. Investment and the development that results will occur only under conditions with minimal financial risk. Latin America has many environmental resources and raw materials upon which to build its economy, but of even greater importance are its human resources—its people. In a free market economy, supported by a stable government and an educated population in which citizens are free to pursue their dreams, prosperity will almost certainly come.

Gazing into a geographical "crystal ball," some areas are a bit hazy. It is difficult to get a clear view of what lies ahead. Today, more than at any time in the region's long history, however, many if not most of the faces are smiling. This sign of optimism, perhaps more than any other factor, suggests that Latin America can look ahead to a bright future.

Pre-12000 B.C.	Earliest evidence of human presence in region; dates vary greatly and some evidence suggests a much earlier presence of perhaps 40,000 years.
5000 B.C.	Evidence of early plant domestication in Mesoamerica and the central Andean area.
3000 B.C.	Caral and other large urban centers in coastal Peru are established.
1500 B.C.	Early civilizations begin to flourish in central and eastern Mexico.
1100 B.C.– A.D. 900	Mayan civilization flourishes in Mesoamerica.
A.D. 200–600	Teotihuacán (Mexico) reaches a population estimated at 125,000 to 200,000, making it the largest urban center in the Americas, and perhaps the world, at that time.
A.D. 200–800	Moche civilization flourishes in northern Peru.
500	Famous Nazca Lines are formed in southern Peru.
1200	Quechua-speaking people begin expanding (and ultimately become the Incas).
1438–1533	Incan civilization and culture expands.
1492	Christopher Columbus lands on the outer Bahamas, perhaps the island of San Salvador (Watling Island).
1519	Hernán Cortés and some 600 soldiers land on east coast of Mexico.
1522	Spanish complete conquest of Aztec Empire.
1531–1533	Francisco Pizarro and a small band of Spaniards conquer vast Inca Empire; Pizarro establishes Lima as his capital in 1535.
1549–1561	Portugal establishes foothold on the fertile Brazilian coastal plain.
1780	Hurricane sweeps Lesser Antilles, killing an estimated 22,000 people (the deadliest hurricane on record).
1800–1820	Most Spanish colonies gain their independence.
1804	Haiti gains independence from France to become the world's first independent black republic.
1902	Eruption of Mount Pelée on Martinique, in the Lesser Antilles, destroys the city of St. Pierre, killing 40,000.
1911	American Hiram Bingham discovers Machu Picchu.

1930s Disease destroys banana industry in Central America.

1935 American pilot Jimmy Angel discovers Angel Falls in the Guiana Highlands, Venezuela.

1939 Earthquake in central Chile damages 50,000 square miles (130,000 square kilometers) and kills 30,000.

1960 Earthquake measuring 9.5 on the Richter scale (the highest ever recorded) strikes off Chile's south-central coast, killing 2,000.

1970 Rock and snow avalanche cascades down Peru's Mount Huascaran, burying villages and taking an estimated 18,000 lives.

1976 Earthquake destroys Guatemala City, Guatemala, leaving an estimated 25,000 dead and one-sixth of the country's population homeless.

1985 Eruption of Colombia's Nevado del Ruiz creates mudslides that bury several towns and leaves 25,000 dead.

BOOKS

Blouet, Brian W., and O. M. Blouet, eds. *Latin America and the Caribbean: A Systematic and Regional Survey.* New York: John Wiley & Sons, 2005.

Brawer, Moshe. *Atlas of South America.* New York: Simon & Schuster, 1991.

Clawson, David L. *Latin America & the Caribbean: Lands and Peoples.* Boston: McGraw-Hill, 2004.

Collier, Simon, Thomas E. Skidmore, and Harold Blakemore, eds. *The Cambridge Encyclopedia of Latin America and the Caribbean.* Cambridge: Cambridge University Press, 1992.

Davidson, William V., and James J. Parsons, eds. *Historical Geography of Latin America.* Baton Rouge, LA: Louisiana State University Press, 1980.

Goodwin, Paul B., ed. *Latin America.* Dubuque, IA: McGraw-Hill/Dushkin, 2004.

Gritzner, Charles F. "Chickens, Worms, and a Little Bull: Some Animated Perspectives on American History," *Journal of Geography* 76, no. 5, (March 1977): pp. 111–112.

James, Preston E., and C. W. Minkel. *Latin America.* New York: John Wiley & Sons, 1986.

Knapp, Gregory (ed.). *Latin America in the Twenty-First Century: Challenges and Solutions.* Austin, TX: University of Texas Press, 2002.

Lombardi, Cathryn L. *Latin American History: A Teaching Atlas.* Madison, WI: The University of Wisconsin Press, 1983.

Richardson, Bonham C. *The Caribbean in the Wider World, 1492–1992: A Regional Geography.* New York: Cambridge University Press, 1992.

West, Robert C., and John P. Augelli. *Middle America: Its Lands and Peoples.* Englewood Cliffs, NJ: Prentice Hall, 1989.

Chelsea House Books on Latin American Countries:

Crooker, Richard A. *Argentina* (2003); *Chile* (2004); *Cuba* (2003); *Venezuela* (2006)

Dendinger, Roger. *Costa Rica* (2003); *Guatemala* (2003)

Greenbaum, Harry. *Brazil* (2003)

Gritzner, Charles F. *Mexico* (2002)

Gritzner, Charles F. & Yvonne. *Peru* (2004)

Gritzner, Janet H. *Jamaica* (2004)

Lineback, Mandy & Jason Gritzner. *Bolivia* (2003)

Lopez, Jose Javier. *Puerto Rico* (2006)

NOTE: For further and current information on Latin American countries or specific topics such as the environment, population, economic, political, social, or other data, please use Internet search engines as appropriate. For example, an excellent general information source for any of the world's countries is *www.cia.gov/cia/publications/factbook* (Latin American countries by name; also rankings of selected data by country for region).

page:

CHARLES F. GRITZNER is Distinguished Professor of Geography at South Dakota State University in Brookings. He is now in his fifth decade of college teaching, scholarly research, and writing. In addition to teaching, he enjoys traveling, writing, working with teachers, and sharing his love of geography with students and readers alike. As Consulting Editor and frequent author for the Chelsea House MODERN WORLD NATIONS and MODERN WORLD CULTURES series, he has a wonderful opportunity to combine each of these "hobbies." His travels have taken him to Latin America on many occasions.

Professionally, Gritzner has served as both President and Executive Director of the National Council for Geographic Education. He has received numerous awards in recognition of his academic and teaching achievements, including the National Council for Geographic Education's George J. Miller Award for Distinguished Service to geography and geographic education.